SOUTH WEST COAST PATH
COAST PATH

Minehead to Padstow

NATIONAL  TRAIL GUIDES

SOUTH WEST COAST PATH

Minehead to Padstow

Roland Tarr

*Photographs by
Mike Williams*

Aurum

in association with

NATURAL
ENGLAND

Acknowledgements

My thanks to the following organisations and people for help and advice:
Tim Parish and Jim Webber, Exmoor National Park; Ben Totterdell of the
Northern Devon Heritage Coast; Simon Ford of the National Trust;
Rebecca and Charlie David and Tim Dingle of North Cornwall Coast and
Countryside; Sarah Welton and Joan Edwards for the article on marine
wildlife; and Peter Woodward for checking historical information.

Roland Tarr was born and brought up in West Somerset and has close family
ties with Exmoor. He was Heritage Coast Officer in Dorset from 1974 to 1988.

This revised edition first published 2009 by Aurum Press Ltd,
7 Greenland Street, London NW1 0ND, www.aurumpress.co.uk
in association with Natural England
Text copyright © 1990, 1997, 2001, 2004, 2007, 2009 by Aurum Press Ltd
and Natural England
Photograph on page 68 copyright © Roland Tarr; all other photographs
copyright © 1990, 1997, 2001, 2004, 2007 by Natural England

A catalogue record for this book is available from the British Library.

ISBN 978 1 84513 464 8

Book design by Robert Updegraff
Printed and bound in Italy by Printer Trento Srl

Cover photograph: *Pentire Point*
Title-page photograph: *Ilfracombe Harbour*

CONTENTS

Circular walks appear on pages 28, 56, 66, 120, 128, 159

HOW TO USE THIS GUIDE

The 630-mile (1008-kilometre) South West Coast Path is covered by four National Trail guides. Each guide describes a section of the path between major estuaries. This book describes the path from Minehead to Padstow, 166 miles (266 kilometres). This guide is in three parts:

• The introduction, historical background to the area and advice for walkers.

• The path itself, described in thirteen chapters, with maps opposite each route description. This part of the guide also includes information on places of interest as well as a number of related short walks, starting either from the path itself or at a car park. Key sites are numbered in the text and on the maps to make it easy to follow the route description.

• The last part includes useful information, such as local transport, accommodation, organisations involved with the path, and further reading.

The maps have been prepared by the Ordnance Survey using 1:25 000 Explorer® maps as a base. The line of the Coast Path is shown in yellow, with the status of each section of the Coast Path – footpath or bridleway for example – shown in green underneath (see key on inside front cover). These rights-of-way markings also indicate the precise alignment of the path at the time of the original surveys, but in some cases the yellow line on these maps may show a route which is different from that shown by those older surveys, and in such cases walkers are recommended to follow the yellow route in this guide, which will be the route that is waymarked with the distinctive acorn symbol 🌰 used for all National Trails. Any parts of the path that may be difficult to follow on the ground are clearly highlighted in the route description, and important points to watch for are marked with letters in each chapter, both in the text and on the maps. *Some maps start on a right-hand page and continue on the left-hand page – black arrows (➤) at the edge of the maps indicate the start point.* Should there have been a need to alter the route since publication of this guide for any reason, walkers are advised to follow the waymarks or signs which have been put up on site to indicate this. Since the Coast Path passes through a military exercise area at Braunton Burrows, walkers are advised to pay particular heed to any signs posted and flags flying relating to entry to the area when firing is taking place.

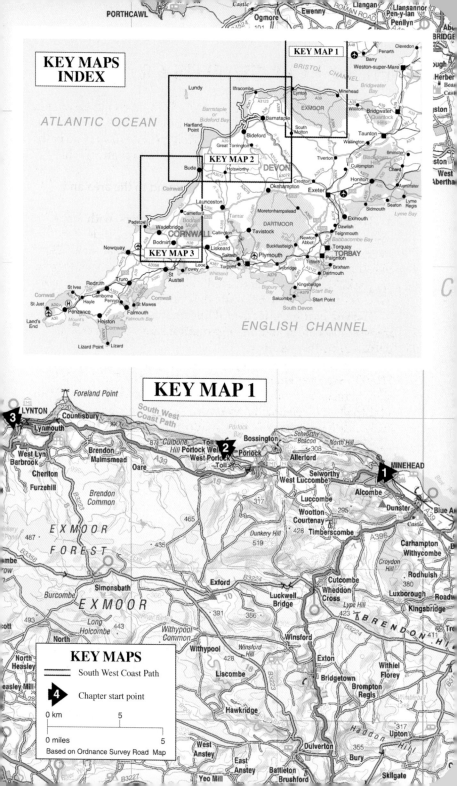

KEY MAPS INDEX

KEY MAP 1

KEY MAP 2

KEY MAP 3

KEY MAP 1

KEY MAPS

—— South West Coast Path

▶ Chapter start point

0 km   5

0 miles   5

Based on Ordnance Survey Road Map

North West Point

Tibbett's Point

LUNDY

Rat Island

South West Point Surf Point

KEY MAP 2

Ferries to Lundy depart from:	
Bideford	2 hrs 15mins
Ilfracombe (Summer only)	2 hrs
Clovelly (Summer only)	1 hr

0 km   5

0 miles   5

Based on Ordnance Survey Road Map

BARNSTAPLE
OR
BIDEFORD
BAY

HARTLAND POINT

Titchberry   Windbury Point

Stoke   Higher Clovelly   Clovelly   Fai No

Hartland Quay   Hartland   Buck's Mills

Milford   Philham   Clovelly Dykes   Ho

Elmscott   Edistone   Tosberry   Buck's Cross Cranford

South Hole   Woolfardisworthy or Woolsery   Parkham As

Knaps Longpeak   Welcombe   Alminstone Cross

Meddon   Ashmansworthy

Gooseham   Eastcott   Youlstone   Dinworthy   East Putf

Morwenstow   Shop   West Putfor

Higher Sharpnose Point   Colscott   Bradworthy   Haylown

Woodford   Abb Bick

Lower Sharpnose Point   Coombe   Sutcombe

Thurdon   Alfardisworthy

Kilkhampton   Soldon Cross

Stibb

Lana   Holswort Beacon

BUDE   Poughill   Beechworthy

Flexbury   Grimscott

Bude Haven   STRATTON   Pancrasweek   Holsworthy

BUDE   Launcells   Staddon

BAY   Jewell's Marhamchurch Cross   Bridgerule   Holla

Pyworthy   Whimble

Widemouth Bay   Chasty

Titson

The Valley of The Rocks

ILFRACOMBE   A399   159   Hele   Combe Martin   Heddon's Mouth   Trentishoe   Martinhoe   Toll   316
Bull Point   Lee   206   Berrynarbor   Heale   Kemacott   East Ilkerton
Rockham Bay   Mortehoe   Lincombe   Slade   Parracombe   Shallowford
Morte Point   A361   A3123   269   A399   Kentisbury   Blackmoor Gate   480
Woolacombe   B3343   Trimstone   262   Patchole   Kentisbury Ford   Arlington   337   Knightacott   Challacombe   Shoulsbarrow Common
Morte Bay   199   210   West Down   East Down   Clifton   Arlington Beccott   Arlington Court   329   Leworthy
Point   Pickwell   North Buckland   Georgeham   Bittadon   Milltown   Muddiford   194   Loxhore   Bratton Fleming   Benton   Lydcott
Croyde Bay   158   Knowle   Halsinger   Marwood   Guineaford   198   Shirwell   Stoke Rivers   Heas
Croyde   Lobb   Pippacott   Prixford   Kingsheanton   A39   Goodleigh   Gunn   West Buckland   Charles   High Bray
Saunton   Braunton   Heanton Punchardon   Ashford   169   BARNSTAPLE   265   East Buckland
Bideford Bar   Wrafton Toll   Chivenor   A361   Newport   Westacott   Landkey   Brayford
Braunton Burrows   Fremington   Bickington   Lake   Little Pill   Swimbridge   Fifleigh
Appledore   Yelland   Instow   Bickleton   Tawstock   Bishop's Tawton   A361
ward Ho!   Northam   A39   Westleigh   St John's Chapel   Chapelton   Cobbaton   Chittlehampton   146   SOU MOLT
BIDEFORD   Eastleigh   Newton Tracey   Ensis   Herner   B3227   B3226   George Nympton   158   Alswe
obbotsham   Ford   Woodtown   East-the-Water   Woodtown   Hiscott   Alverdiscott   Fishleigh Barton   Umberleigh   Clapworthy   173   Romansle
worthy   Littleham   Landcross   Gammaton   Yarnscombe   Atherington   Warkleigh   Satterleigh   Chittlehamholt   King's Nympton   Cadbury Barton
am   Weare Giffard   Huntshaw   Langridgeford   Sherwood Green   High Bickington   Portsmouth Arms Sta   King's Nympton Sta   Elstone
Buckland Brewer   Monkleigh   Dartington Glass Factory   High Bullen   St Giles in the Wood   Northcote Manor   Chulmleigh
Frithelstock Stone   Frithelstock   GREAT TORRINGTON   Kingscott   Roborough   B3096   Copy Lake
tibb Cross   Langtree   Little Torrington   Beaford   Burrington   Ashreigney   Bridge Reeve   Eggesford Sta   B9042
rthy   A386   Peters Marland   Winswell   A3124   Riddlecombe   East Ashley   Brushford   Coldridge   Nymet Rowland
Newton St Petrock   Woollaton   Merton   Huish   Dolton   Hollocombe   Wembworthy   East Leigh
amerel   171   Dowland   Zeal Monachorum
Shebbear   Buckland Filleigh   Petrockstowe   Meeth   138   Iddesleigh   Winkleigh   Honeychurch   North Tawton   204   Dow
Thornbury   Bradford   Ash Barton   Sheepwash   134   Broadwoodkelly   B3220
Black Torrington   175   Highampton   Monkokehampton   B3217
Holemoor   13   Graddon Moor   A3072   Hatherleigh   Jacobstowe   Exbourne   A3072
Brandis Corner   193   Halwill   142   A386   Sampford
A3079

KEY MAP 3

0 km 5
0 miles 5

Based on Ordnance Survey Road Map

Distance checklist

This list will assist you in calculating the distances between places on the Coast Path where you may be planning to stay overnight, or in checking your progress along the way.

location	approx. distance from previous location	
	miles	km
Minehead	0.0	0
Bossington	6.0	9.7
Porlock Weir	2.9	4.6
Culbone	1.7	2.8
Lynmouth Harbour	10.3	16.6
Lynton	0.4	0.7
Combe Martin	13.3	21.4
Ilfracombe	5.3	8.6
Woolacombe	8.5	13.7
Saunton	8.6	13.9
Braunton	6.3	10.2
Barnstaple (Long Bridge)	5.4	8.7
Instow (for Ferry to Appledore)	7.4	11.9
Bideford	2.7	4.4
Appledore	3.5	5.6
Westward Ho!	4.8	7.7
Buck's Mills	6.8	10.9
Clovelly	4.3	7
Hartland Point	7.4	11.9
Hartland Quay	2.9	4.6
Devon / Cornwall county boundary	5.7	9.2
Bude (canal lock)	9.5	15.3
Crackington Haven	9.8	15.8
Boscastle Harbour	6.7	10.8
Rocky Valley	2.7	4.4
Tintagel Haven	2.0	3.2
Trebarwith Strand	2.2	3.5
Port Gaverne	6.2	9.9
Port Isaac	0.7	1.2
Portquin	3.2	5.1
Pentire Point	4.0	6.4
Polzeath	1.7	2.8
Rock (Ferry to Padstow)	2.9	4.6

PREFACE

The South West Coast Path National Trail is a 630-mile (1008-km) adventure around the coastline of the south-west peninsula. From Minehead on the edge of the Exmoor National Park all the way to the shores of Poole Harbour, it is simply the best way to enjoy this wonderful coastline, its scenery, wildlife and history.

The section of the Trail between Minehead and Padstow is perhaps the most varied of the four described in the complete set of these guidebooks. It takes in the hog's-back cliffs of Exmoor, dramatic cliffs and headlands (including Great Hangman, the highest point on the Path), the ever-changing Taw-Torridge and Camel estuaries and the vast dune system at Braunton Burrows – one of only 13 Biosphere Reserves in the UK.

Following the Coast Path you can go at your own pace, enjoying the changing landscape and wildlife and getting the feel of how people have lived and worked in the coastal corridor down the centuries. You may also stop off at busy towns and villages, bustling resorts, beaches or sheltered coves – each with its own character.

Natural England is proud of its role in creating and being the major funder of the South West Coast Path. The Path is maintained by local authorities, working with other organisations such as the National Trust where appropriate. One of the family of 15 National Trails in England and Wales, the Coast Path is clearly signed with the acorn waymark. It is enjoyed by millions of people every year, both local residents and visitors, and offers relaxation and challenge, tranquillity and inspiration. Whether you are about to stroll out on the cliffs from Westward Ho! or Tintagel, or walk all the way from Minehead to Padstow, I hope you too will discover – or rediscover – the endless fascination of the South West Coast Path.

Martin Doughty
Chair
Natural England

PART ONE

INTRODUCTION

INTRODUCTION

by John Macadam

On the edge of the land

The South West Coast Path must be one of the most spectacular and varied long-distance trails in the world. And at 630 miles (just over 1000 kilometres), from Minehead to Poole, it is certainly Britain's longest. Never far from the sea, the route will take the walker high above the shore and then swoop down to a fishing village in a cove. In fact, someone has calculated that if you walk those 630 miles, you will also climb almost four times the height of Everest! Not that you will need extra oxygen, of course, though windproof insulated clothing can be much appreciated if you are walking into a sou'westerly gale. At other times a T-shirt is more appropriate. But more about that later.

The trail will take you through historic towns and villages, through woods, fields and sand dunes, and alongside quiet creeks and past streams falling from high cliffs into the sea. Occasionally you will walk through a busy town, but often there will be more wildlife – the inevitable gulls, but maybe also seals, basking sharks, dolphins or choughs – than humans. To refresh yourself there are local beers, clotted-cream teas, Cornish pasties, Ruby Red steaks and Dorset Blue cheese, and smoked mackerel. Or you could sample the industrial heritage: pilchard 'palaces' and mining in Cornwall, or quarrying on Portland. If none of that takes your fancy, there are more ethereal pleasures: literary associations, from Daniel Defoe to John Fowles, connections with artists from Turner to Kurt Jackson, the Cornish language ('Kernewek') and innumerable Celtic saints. And if you do not like beer, there's a range of ciders made from traditional varieties of apples in Somerset and Devon, and even a few recently planted vineyards near the Path.

For centuries, local people would have used paths along the coast for many purposes, including gathering food and looking for wreckage. But in the 18th century the government imposed high import duties on a range of luxury goods, precipitating a rapid growth in smuggling – and yet another use for the paths. The official response was draconian legislation prohibiting anyone from 'lurking, waiting or loitering within five miles from the sea-coast', but the trade was too lucrative to suppress. Finally, in the early 19th century, the coastguard service was set up, with men patrolling nightly, and so a continuous coast path developed. The coastguards had to be able to look down into coves and narrow inlets, so their route was truly at the edge of the cliffs. But by the early 1800s, a few visitors were using the path for leisure, even if they sometimes had to prove that they had no other purpose!

Use of much of this path was lost, not, as might be expected, by natural geological processes, but by landowners, often backed by the courts, prohibiting access. In 1949 the Act which set up National Parks in England and Wales also set up long-distance paths, including one around the South West Peninsula. The Path was opened in stages, with the last major section opened in 1978, and the patient operation to reinstate the route along the coast is now nearly complete.

The driftwood-built Parson Hawker's hut, Vicarage Cliff, Morwenstow, where he wrote some of his poetry.

The Packhorse Bridge at Allerford.

Geological processes have indeed destroyed the old coast-guards' tracks in many places, and those same processes are no respecters of hard-won modern routes, so realignment is an ongoing task. Active erosion also means that the geology is exposed in many places, not clothed in soil and vegetation as inland, so the walker will see an impressive range of strata, folds, faults, intrusions, stacks and caves – a real *tour de force*. Indeed, a 95-mile stretch of the coast, in East Devon and Dorset, is designated a World Heritage Site for the global scientific importance of its exposure of 185 million years of the Mesozoic Era. This is the icing on the cake, for much of the Path passes through areas with one or more national designations for landscape, wildlife or geology: National Park, National Nature Reserve, Heritage Coast, Area of Outstanding Natural Beauty, Site of Special Scientific Interest, and others. But you do not have to be an expert (or understand all these designations!) to enjoy all the flowers, butterflies and birds you will see at different times of the year.

Management of the Path requires great sensitivity to potentially competing interests. Funded primarily by Natural England, this task is shared between approximately 70 staff working for six highway authorities (or their agents), the Ministry of Defence, and the National Trust, and co-ordinated by the South West Coast Path Team based in Exeter. Day-to-day work includes cutting back vegetation, clearing drainage ditches, and replacing broken stiles and signs. In addition to routine maintenance, South West Coast Path managers strive to provide the best experience by realigning sections that involve road walking or re-routing the Path as quickly as possible after cliff-falls have taken place.

Planning your walk

You may be planning to walk the whole length of the Path, or you may just intend to walk a short distance. Even a walk along the promenade is likely to be a walk along the Coast Path! Some of the Path can be enjoyed by people who are less mobile, but very little can be used by cyclists or horse-riders.

If you are planning short walks, there are many circular routes to get you back to your starting point, and in many places there is public transport (but make sure you take the bus or train to your furthest point, then walk back, or else leave yourself plenty of time).

Whatever walk you plan, be sure you are fit enough, particularly if you are planning to walk for several days consecutively. Remember those three Everests! Some people walk the whole Path in one go, and most take 50–60 days to do this. A few people have taken far less time, but they must have missed out a great deal.

The best time to walk the Path is probably May–June, with long days, masses of wild flowers and few people. Another good time is September, when most of the summer visitors have gone. Since the area relies heavily on tourism, there is a wide range of accommodation, from campsites, youth hostels, B&Bs (bed & breakfast) to rather grand hotels, though everywhere can become full at the height of the tourist season in July and August and it is wise to book ahead. If you intend to camp away from a recognised campsite, you will need to ask permission of the landowner, usually the local farmer, and remember to leave no trace of your stay.

If you plan to walk between October and April, you may have the luxury of the Coast Path to yourself. You may also find some ferries are not running and public services, like buses and trains, are running a restricted winter schedule. Tourist Information Centres (TICs), the information section at the back of this book and the National Trail website (www.nationaltrail.co.uk) will either provide the necessary information or give you the necessary contacts.

Equipment

British weather is notorious for its changeability, and the weather in the South West is generally wetter, windier and warmer than most of Britain. Most of the Coast Path is very exposed to the elements; the exceptions are some of the estuaries. The relative exposure depends on which way the wind is coming from – the prevailing wind is southwesterly – and which way the coast faces. The effects of windchill can be extreme: windchill is caused by the wind evaporating moisture from your skin.

With all this in mind, it makes sense to get a weather forecast (from the media, by telephone or the web) and be prepared. It is always sensible to carry a windproof waterproof: the breathable ones are best, and the reproofable ones with a lifetime guarantee are the best of all.

There are various types of walking trousers, though most people use quick-drying polycotton fabrics, with waterproof overtrousers. Denim is decidedly unwise as when wet it becomes stiff and heavy, and is also very slow to dry, thus increasing the risk of hypothermia. A hat of some form is recommended, and a supply of sunscreen to be applied in good time to your neck, arms and anywhere else that is exposed. Traditionally, strong shoes or walking boots with good grips have always been recommended, though some people are very happy wearing sandals designed for walkers.

Finally, walkers need to take an adequate supply of liquid, a whistle and a first-aid kit, all in a rucksack which is adjusted to fit the wearer comfortably. Of course, long-distance walkers will have far more to carry than this, but will take trouble to minimise the weight. Some companies and B&B owners will transport your pack for you to your next stop, for a fee, so that all you need to carry is a daypack. Cash machines are only to be found in the larger towns, so paying bills and withdrawing cash can be a problem, especially for visitors without a sterling cheque account.

Finding your way

The sign for all National Trails is a stylised acorn, and you will find this cut into wooden waymarks, chiselled into stone waymarks, cast in metal, and stuck to aluminium road signs. Most signs also bear the words 'Coast Path'.

You should have few problems following the acorns and thus the trail. The route is also shown on the maps in this

St Nectan's Glen.

guidebook. You may find that the route has changed from that shown on the maps, in which case follow the acorns and any diversion signs. The reason for the latter may well be a cliff-fall, or the Path starting to crumble away. It is obviously foolhardy to ignore diversion signs.

Safety

The main safety message is: keep to the Path. The Path is close to the edge of the cliff in many places. Make sure you are suitably equipped both for your walk and for changing weather conditions.

Those who go down to beaches and rocks beside the sea need to be aware of the tides, with around 9 metres between high and low tide at Minehead, though only a couple of metres at Poole. Every year people get cut off by the tide and have to be rescued. People also get washed off rocks by so-called 'freak waves'. At many places around this coastline you can watch surfers waiting for the bigger waves.

Bathing too can be hazardous, chiefly because of currents. It is best only to swim in safe areas patrolled by lifeguards, who are employed only in the summer. Many beaches have rip currents which drain most of the water that comes onto the beach. If you get caught in a rip current, do not try to swim against it, but rather swim diagonally across it until you are in stiller water, when it is safe to swim back to the beach.

If you do get into difficulties on the Path, the international alarm call is six long blasts on a whistle, followed by one minute's silence.

The coastguards are responsible for dealing with any emergency that occurs on the coast or at sea. Please remember that there are no coastguard lookouts now, and the service relies on the watchful eyes of the public. If you see vessels or people you think are in distress, dial 999 (or 112 on a mobile) and ask for the coastguard. Beneath some cliffs there may be no mobile signal.

The Act forbidding 'lurking, waiting or loitering within five miles from the sea-coast' was repealed in 1825, so relax, explore and enjoy the South West Coast Path and the coasts of Somerset, Devon, Cornwall and Dorset.

PART TWO

SOUTH WEST COAST PATH
Minehead to Padstow

1 Minehead to Porlock Weir

passing Bossington
9¹/₂ miles (14.5 km)

The Coast Path starts from Minehead seafront between the station and the harbour **1**, just past the Red Lion Hotel. A pair of hands gripping an open Coast Path map emerges from the ground to celebrate the official start and end of the 630-mile (1008-km) path.

From the hands the original route went up the donkey track between the cottages opposite and headed west in the lovely coastal woods, giving glimpses of the harbour, to the top of North Hill. The Coast Path official route now heads west along

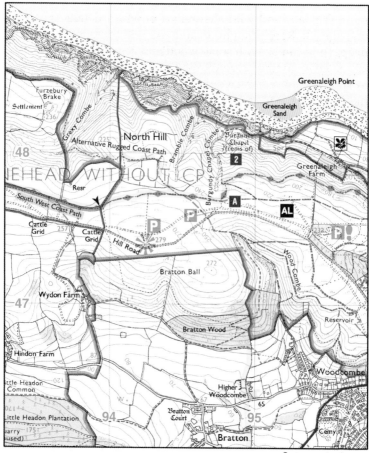

Contours are given in metres
The vertical interval is 10m

the seafront pavement past the harbour. Take care where there is no pavement. Follow the tarmac path beside the pebble beach up to the end of the wide grass lawn ($\frac{1}{2}$ mile / 1 km). Take the narrow cliff-top path and where it divides keep west and use the path closest to the cliff top. Exercise caution and keep away from the extreme edge, which overhangs in places. Join a wider track by a phone pole and then the part tarmac access road west to Greenaleigh Farm. As you come into sight of the farm, steps take you to an uphill woodland path that doubles back sharply to join with a bridleway (turn right) to North Hill.

As the steep path from Burgundy Chapel **2** joins from the right (north), the Coast Path turns briefly inland for a hundred yards and then turns right at the next junction to continue due west **A**. At the next junction after that leave the more rugged clifftop route to the seaward side (unless you intend to take this more dramatic and wild alternative, of which details are given on page 28). Keep straight on and you will come into sight of a deep, wide combe with some woodland running up the middle and smaller combes dividing from it. Go through a bridlegate to keep inland of the green grassy area ahead and stay just to the landward side of the fields for 2 miles (3 km). You will be able to see Dunkery Beacon to the south-west and Selworthy

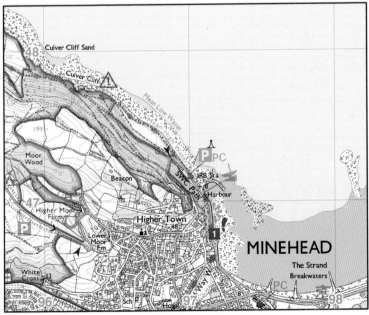

Contours are given in metres
The vertical interval is 10m

23

Beacon behind you. The farmhouses at West Myne and East Myne are now deserted, but you will see on the map their two names, pronounced in West Somerset dialect as Main. 'Mynedd' is hill in Welsh, hence the name Minehead.

When you come to a track leading to a car park across to the left (south) you are north of Selworthy **3**. Fork right and keep along the shoulder until the path divides, go down through the middle of a dry valley (Hurlstone Combe) with gorse and heather slopes to the cliff edge, and there branch left (south) to walk half a mile (1 km) to Bossington. At Bossington there are cream teas and

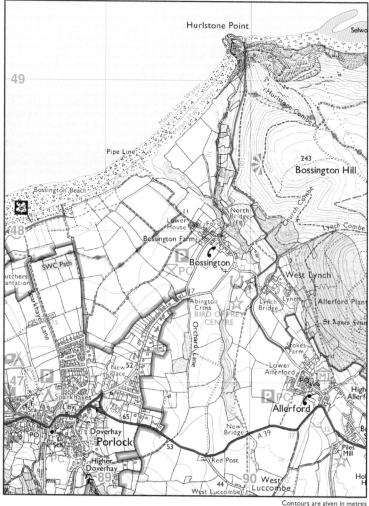

Contours are given in metres
The vertical interval is 10m

accommodation. Just to the south-east of Bossington is Lynch, where there is a Chapel of Ease **4**, built around 1530.

In 1996 the shingle ridge across Porlock Bay, along which the Coast Path used to run, was breached by a storm. This has resulted in the fields immediately behind the ridge being inundated each high tide. The Coast Path now runs around the edge of the marsh, roughly following the new high tide mark. As huge volumes of water flow in and out through the narrow breach each tide, it is not safe to try and walk along the length of the shingle ridge.

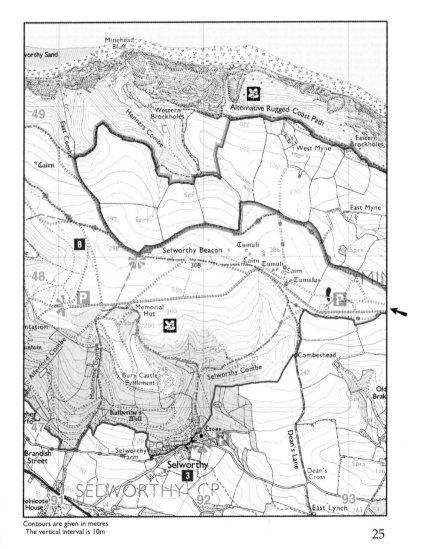

Contours are given in metres
The vertical interval is 10m

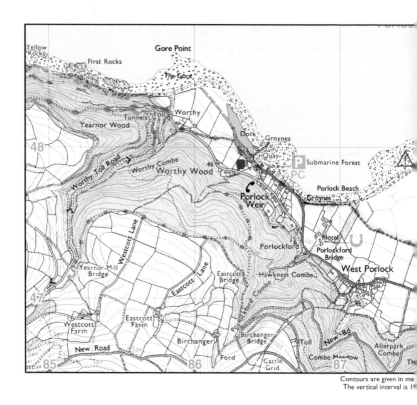

Contours are given in me
The vertical interval is 1

Crossing Porlock Bay

From the NT car park in Bossington, go seawards down the village street past the cream and chocolate thatched cottages. Continue past Lower House Farm along the stone track until you come to the second turning left some 50 yards past Lower House. Turn left and step over the normally tiny trackside stream to follow a long straight track going south-west and enclosed by ancient hedges. Where the hedges were removed some years ago they have been recently replaced. Where the new planting comes to an end, on the parish boundary, turn right along the field boundary going briefly towards the sea. A new fence then guides you westwards and then seawards again to meet a path which leads from Porlock to the pebble beach. Go straight across this path. When very high tides occur this section may be flooded. If this appears to be the case as you arrive here, go up to Porlock, follow signs for the toll road just

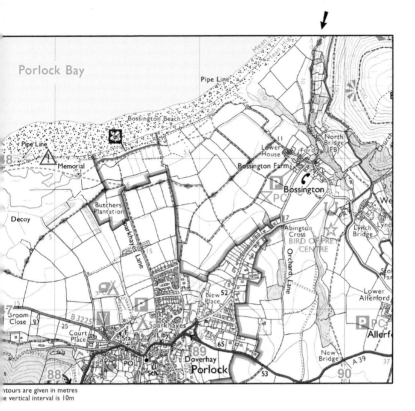

Porlock Bay

Pipe Line

Bossington Beach

Pipe Line

Memorial

Butchers Plantation

Decoy

Sparkhayes Lane

Lower House

Ford

North Bridge (FB)

Bossington Farm

Bossington

PC

Abington Cross

BIRD OF PREY CENTRE

Orchard Lane

Lynch Bridge

Lower Allerford

Broom Close

B 3225

Court Place

New Place

New 52

65

Sparkhayes

Lib'y

89

Doverhay

Porlock

Sch

PO

53

New Bridge

A 39

90

Allerf'

88

itours are given in metres
e vertical interval is 10m

past the village hall and turn right off that toll road to follow the signed footpath through the woods to Porlock Weir.

Web addresses for tide tables for Porlock Bay and other key locations along this part of the Coast Path are given in 'Useful Information' (page 162).

To continue, keep going west on one side or other of the fences running parallel with the beach until you meet a path which goes to central Porlock through meadows beside Sparkhayes Lane. Turn right towards the sea for a few yards and re-enter NT land.

Continue to follow the field boundaries round the edge of the marshes parallel to the sea, and cross the bridge across the stream which drove the mills of Porlock. Carry straight ahead on the seaward side of the hedge and wall. Finally, where the footpath from West Porlock joins from the left, carry straight on. Walk along the pebble beach and join the road up concrete steps. Just down the road (take care, as there is no footway) are the lovely harbour and harbour side pubs of Porlock Weir.

A Circular Clifftop Walk on Bossington Hill
or the alternative rugged Coast Path route from Minehead to Bossington

6½ miles (10.6 km)

If you want to make the main Coast Path and alternative rugged route into a round walk, park at the National Trust car park above Combeshead and go north along one of the tracks across open country until you come to the Coast Path and the fence surrounding the green fields of East and West Myne. Turn right (east) and follow the track until you reach a grassy path leading towards the sea.

If you are already on the Path and intend to make the alternative rugged route your choice for proceeding west, branch right soon after the path junction above Burgundy Chapel (Burgundy Chapel Combe). In either case you will come to a gate giving access to the area of grassland. Go through the gate, then straight ahead and left down through the gorse and right to follow the landward side of a gully. Make your way gradually down the bracken- and gorse-covered combe before you. Soon you will be overlooking Grexy Combe and the junction of two streams,

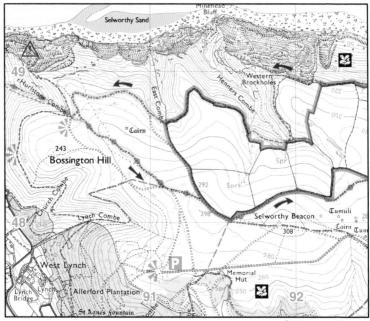

Contours are given in metres
The vertical interval is 10m

which you cross, rising steeply west, keeping a fence and traditional stone wall to your left when you get to the top.

One mile (1.6 km) along this route yet another deep combe opens before you. Turn inland to go round it, keeping more or less on the level before dropping briefly but steeply to cross the stream below. Then keep once more parallel to the coast before crossing another small stream and returning north-westwards to the clifftop slopes. Directly across the Bristol Channel you may identify the white lighthouse at Nash Point, on the Glamorgan Heritage Coast.

Skirt round the back of East Combe, a hanging valley, keeping close to the field boundary, to a wicket gate and turn once again seaward, keeping your height or rising slightly to follow the track along the top western edge. After leaving this steep coastal combe, keep parallel to the sea and westwards to rejoin the main Coast Path.

(If you want to do this as a round walk, fork right at the 'Rugged Coast Path' sign and left where a track skirts around North Hill. Go straight through the gate and descend left into the combe now before you. Then walk back 2 miles (3 km) to the car park where you started, following the carved wooden Coast Path signs.)

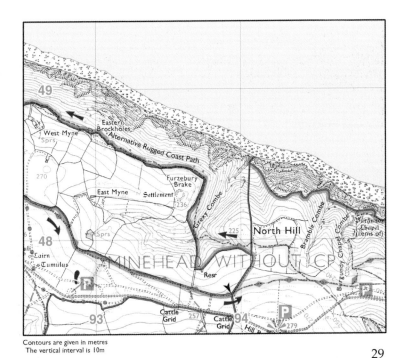

Contours are given in metres
The vertical interval is 10m

Conserving the north coasts of Somerset, Devon and Cornwall

The Coast Path is officially looked after by the relevant local authority and Natural England reimburses a percentage of the costs. Natural England is the government-financed organisation responsible for conserving the countryside and improving access and facilities for people to enjoy it, following on the work of the former Countryside Commission/Agency which played a vital role in linking all the footpaths which go together to make up the South West Coast Path.

English Nature has been the official organisation responsible for the conservation of the flora and fauna and geologically important sites throughout England, and for advising the government on relevant subjects. Sites of Special Scientific Interest have been designated by them and strict guidelines laid down for their protection. Many areas along this path are designated as SSSIs. English Nature has also established and managed National Nature reserves. Since 2006 all these activities have come within the sphere of Natural England.

Natural England also now covers the new grants systems for agricultural land. This should help all those involved in conservation, recreation, food production and other local economic activity to work together with the same aims. Much sought-after grants are available under the 'Entry Level Scheme', 'Higher Level Stewardship' and 'Organic Entry Level Stewardship'. These grants can, for example, be used to give additional access, guard ancient monuments by not ploughing them, plant new hedges and woodlands, further reduce spraying regimes and manage wildlife.

Farmers and landowners are therefore able to consider the possibility of switching part of their activities towards creating a greener future and a more pleasant environment for those who come to enjoy the coast and countryside. This should in turn create a healthier population who will have better opportunities to carry out open-air activities such as riding, cycling and walking. The economic benefits of this green tourism are considerable, and result in a direct increase in local employment and incomes, much needed after the changes of recent years.

The county wildlife trusts, the British Trust for Conservation (BTCV) and the Royal Society for the Protection of Birds (RSPB) give help and advice. Co-operation between landowners, farmers, local authorities, the Exmoor National Park Authority and

Northern Devon and North Cornwall Coast and Countryside services, the various civic amenity and civic societies of towns and villages along the route, and hundreds of individuals, has been a prime factor in the successful protection of this coast.

The Coast Path lies within the Exmoor National Park from Minehead to Combe Martin and passes through the UK's first functioning UNESCO Biosphere Reserve, an area designated by the United Nations because of the importance of its ecology and centred on the Sand Dune System at Braunton Burrows. The Biosphere area reaches between Exmoor and Cornwall and is co-ordinated by the Northern Devon Coast and Countryside Service. Much of the North Devon Coast is also recognised as one of our finest landscapes and is designated as an Area of Outstanding Natural Beauty.

The National Park exists to conserve and enhance the natural beauty, wildlife and cultural heritage of Exmoor and to promote opportunities for the understanding and enjoyment of the special qualities of Exmoor by the public. To this end the National Park Authority works with other organisations whilst protecting and improving the social and economic well-being of the local population.

The Northern Devon and North Cornwall Heritage Coast and Countryside Service co-ordinate paid staff and volunteers in a wide range of similar conservation and information work, with a strong emphasis on local involvement and consultation, practical action and protection through planning policies. The Tarka Trail consists of 180 miles (288 km) of footpath, bridleway and rail link connecting locations in Henry Williamson's novel *Tarka the Otter*. The Trail passes through a rich variety of countryside, the saltmarsh of the Taw and Torridge estuaries, and through valleys of ancient woodland. The 32 miles (30 km) of trail between Braunton and Meeth follow a disused railway, reopened in 1992 as a cycle/walkway.

The National Trust was founded in 1895 as a non-profit-making voluntary association, independent of government, to acquire and protect land and buildings of national importance. In 1965 the Trust launched Enterprise Neptune, the aim of which was to acquire the most beautiful stretches of coastline. Their action is complementary to that of the other organisations mentioned here, which work with all the owners and occupiers, whilst the National Trust and their Enterprise Neptune give that added protection which only ownership can ensure.

Long Island, Trevalga, from Trewethett.

2 Porlock Weir to Lynmouth Harbour

via Culbone
12 miles (19.3 km)

At Porlock Weir go up behind the Anchor Hotel, through a gate and straight on along the side of the field behind red-tiled former stables, joining a path which comes up from the harbour.

Go through another gate at the western end of the field and follow the landward side of a hedge to a gate. Then keep to the higher side of a triangular field to the gate at the far end and join a lane. Follow this lane straight ahead (west) until you come to the arches of the Worthy Combe Toll Lodge. Go through the right-hand archway gate and follow the estate ride.

You go by whimsical arched grottoes and turreted lookouts. These were the creation of Lord Lovelace, who spent time in Italy and was inspired by the romantic landscapes there. The well-signed path soon zig-zags back up through the steep slope of the woods to join a much higher track west **A** (right) to Culbone with a further short diversion at **B** before continuing west along an original path.

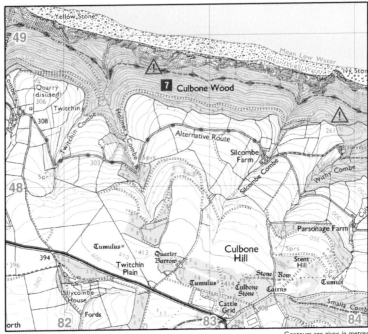

Contours are given in metres
The vertical interval is 10m

Eventually you will see Culbone Church **5** (see page 45) down below, accompanied by the sound of the small stream tumbling down to the sea. This is the smallest complete parish church in England, being only 35 feet long and 12 feet 4 inches wide in the nave. From the church you now have a choice of two routes which you can follow for the next stretch of the Coast Path. Both routes cross the stream by the stone arched bridge and continue straight ahead.

At the time of writing the lower, woodland route follows the permissive path from point **6** past a gate and through Culbone Wood. But if you aim to walk between Minehead and Lynmouth over two days, you may opt to take the higher path, which forks sharp left towards the inland route which offers superb views of Wales and the Exmoor hill farms. This path leads past the B&B at Silcombe Farm, roughly midway between Minehead and Lynton, which is signed for Silcombe. This higher track doubles back and follows the valley upstream from Culbone church. Follow the bridleway west above the deep valley of Withy Combe and join the access road just east of Silcombe. Continue westwards past the farm, crossing Holmer's Combe and Twitchin Combe. Keep to the

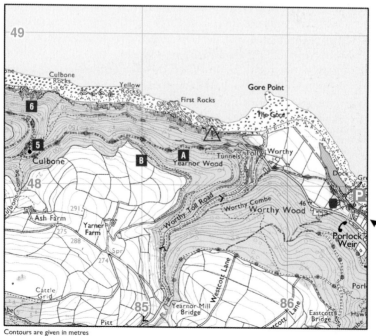

Contours are given in metres
The vertical interval is 10m

seaward side of Broomstreet Farm through the farmyard. The track soon turns to keep parallel with the coast and where all trace of it disappears there is a grassy field before you. Go into the field and turn immediately seawards to go through a gap at the lowest end. Make a steep descent to cross the stream and then keep seawards, rising slightly to the top of the steep western banks of Wheatham Combe. Continue seawards at the top of the steep slope and into the coastal woodland on the cliff slopes. The path turns westwards, parallel to the sea which is some 650 feet (200 metres) below. This is Yenworthy Wood.

You soon emerge into open cliff-slope meadows. Keep up and close to the stone-bank field boundary until it turns inland and up the hill. This point is called Guidhall Corner. Now go away from the boundary and downhill at an angle. First of all the path descends gently through the grass between stunted larch and pine trees before an abrupt descent westwards. The path then zig-zags down to rejoin the woodland Coast Path route from Culbone.

Culbone Woods is an ancient, mainly oak woodland, with whitebeams interspersed into the clearer areas. Exmoor supports seven species of whitebeam, close relatives of the more familiar rowan or mountain ash. All are endemic, that is to say they are not found outside Britain, with three of the species being confined in their world distribution to just the North Devon and Exmoor coast. This makes their conservation here of the utmost importance. They are small shrubs or trees with showy clusters of white flowers in May and berries in autumn which are either red, orange or brown in colour depending on the species. The leaves of some species have a characteristic silvery felt on the under surface which is one of the best ways of spotting them in the dense oak woods that they generally frequent.

The main threat to their survival is through shading out of the sites in which they grow by competing trees and the invasion of rhododendron, which prevents the establishment of the next generation of young whitebeams to replace the old when they die. To reduce this threat the National Park Authority, who own the woods, have been clearing the rhododendron – not an easy job on the steep slopes.

The official path, through Culbone Woods, has experienced several landslips over the years 7, so please be alert to any fresh slippages and, where slips affect the path, follow any diversion signs.

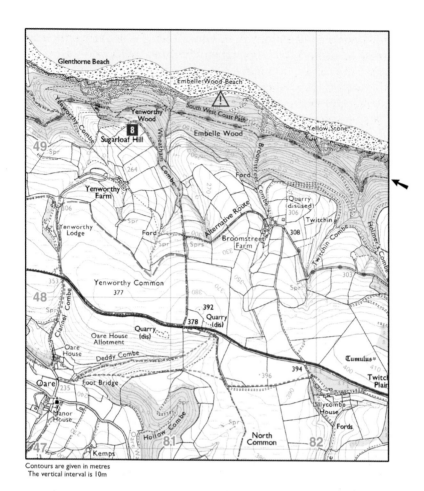

Contours are given in metres
The vertical interval is 10m

The path through the woods is fairly level, with streams cascading down beside the path with seasonal waterfalls in each of the combes you pass by. Read Coleridge's 'Ancient Mariner' and 'Kubla Khan' to find descriptions of the surroundings which were almost certainly inspired by this landscape.

At Yenworthy Wood the path climbs steadily for a few hundred metres, to a path junction **8** where it is joined by the higher route of the Coast Path, which passes Silcombe and Broomstreet Farms, before descending down Wheatam Combe.

From here keep west, contouring along the steep wooded coastal slopes. At the end of this a bridlegate gives access through a wall, where the path continues westwards briefly and then turns sharply inland at the corner of the wall to descend into Yenworthy Combe and cross the stream.

The steadily rising track emerges 400 yards (365 metres) west on a shoulder called Steeple Sturt **9**. Continue westwards and downhill through the woods, cross the stream at Coscombe, and then continue uphill on a forest track. You are now in Devon. Where the track begins to level out look for a small flight of wooden steps on the right, which takes the Coast Path seawards down to Sister's Fountain **10**, a small spring beneath a man-made cairn and rough-hewn slate cross.

Take the path that rises seawards from the fountain until you emerge on a track to pass between a pair of gate pillars surmounted by wild-boar heads. Go to the seaward side of the woodland lodge, with its ornate Victorian window tracery and barge-boards, and keep going along the track. Just before it turns sharply westwards and downhill, the Coast Path mounts a low grassy bank to make its own way westwards towards Wingate Combe, keeping to the contours through the rhododendrons.

Having gone round Wingate Combe, just beneath you and to your right you will see the rocky outcrop of Sir Robert's Chair. Beyond this point the path to the west has fallen away and so the

Lynton and Lynmouth from Countisbury. The earthworks on Wind Hill (centre left) are the remains of Iron Age coastal defences.

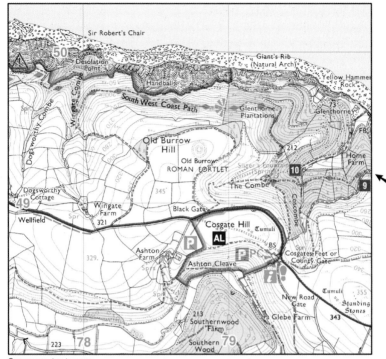

Contours are given in metres
The vertical interval is 10m

route strikes diagonally uphill and inland for 30 to 40 yards on to a shoulder which separates the sea from the wooded banks of the stream flowing down from Desolate Farm. The path turns right (west) and continues up the crest of this shoulder.

(All walkers should be aware of Lyme Disease. The author of this book has contracted it twice with no long term effects. You catch Lyme disease from being bitten by ticks which, as any country walker knows, are everywhere in the countryside. Most ticks are **not** infected with the bacteria that cause Lyme disease, but cases have occasionally been reported in this area. If left untreated, it can infect the heart, joints and nervous system. Most people with Lyme disease develop a reddish skin rash in a ring shape, and this may be the only sign of infection. The rash spreads out from the site of a bite after three to 30 days. Other common symptoms of early Lyme disease include tiredness, headache, joint pains and flu-like symptoms. Early detection and treatment of the disease helps to relieve the symptoms and shorten the illness.)

The Lynmouth Cliff Railway. The weight of water in the tank of the downward car pulls the upward car to the top.

Continuing westwards, keep just to the seaward side of the shoulder. The path then keeps parallel with the sea, to Pudleep Gurt **11**. Swannelcombe **12** follows, with a wealth of ferns, mosses and other greenery lining the tiny miniature waterfalls, followed by Chubhillcombe **13**. Continue to the National Trust omega sign for Glenthome Cliffs, go over the stile beside the gate, then up the grassy track and down, still westwards, until you come to the lighthouse access road (single track) **C**. If you want to have a closer look at the lighthouse **14**, you can reach it by the access road, down through the centre of the dry valley, and then return on the same route to rejoin the Coast Path. The path marked on the map to the west of the lighthouse is very exposed and it is inadvisable to use it in bad weather or strong winds.

Continue down the lighthouse road and over the bridge **D**, and then immediately leave the road to turn away from the sea up a pleasant grassy track, which zig-zags to the right (west) to follow the landward side of the scree-filled valley that dissects the Foreland. You soon come into view of Lynmouth with its harbour, and Lynton above. You can see the water-powered cliff railway, which goes straight up the cliff behind Lynmouth harbour. In the foreground you can see the A39 Minehead–Lynton coast road. The Coast Path runs just below this and then down through the woods into Lynmouth, crosses the harbour, zig- zags across the cliff railway, and then continues west halfway up the cliff slopes of Lynton.

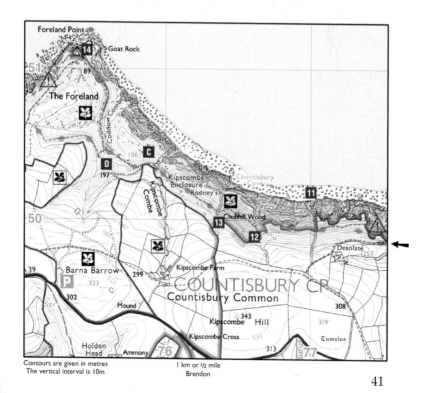

Contours are given in metres
The vertical interval is 10m

1 km or ½ mile
Brendon

Having come into view of Lynmouth, turn left (south-west) along the cliff top, past the gulley called Great Red and then keep to the grassy clifftop path along the edge of Butter Hill. Follow the field boundary stone wall and fence, keeping outside it until you are just below the main road. The path continues just below the main road in a steady descent.

At a National Trust sign, which announces the western end of a 3-mile (5-km) stretch of the path owned by the Trust, you follow the roadside path along the top of a low wall at **E**, 300 yards (275 metres). Then turn seawards down the steep path through the woods, descending the hill in wide sweeping zig-zags to

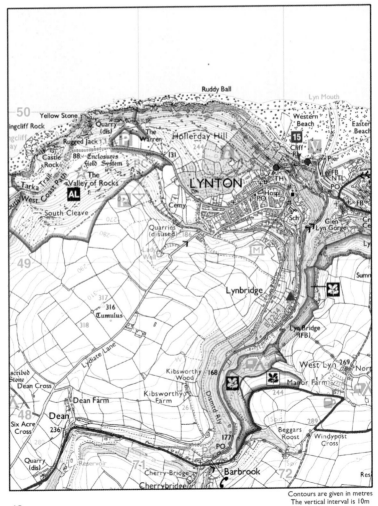

Contours are given in metres
The vertical interval is 10m

descend parallel to the beach on the landward side of a sturdy stone wall. Make one final (right) seaward turn near the bottom, to emerge on a beachside path leading straight towards Lynmouth harbour. Keep left of the Rock House Hotel where a footbridge will take you over to the harbour.

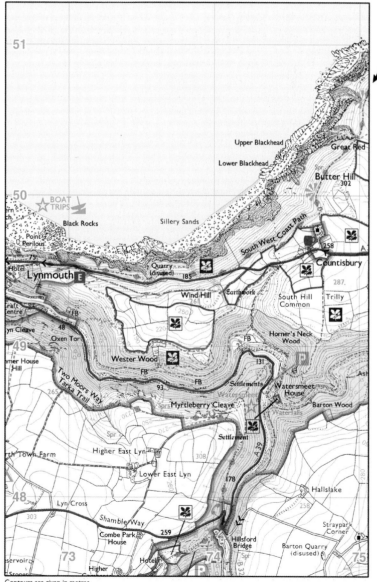

Contours are given in metres
The vertical interval is 10m

The Rhenish Tower at Lynmouth, now a popular tourist site, was originally a sea-water tower.

The smallest complete parish church in England in the village of Culbone.

Culbone Church

The main structure of Culbone Church **5** (see map on page 35) is probably 12th-century with a 13th-century chancel arch. You will find ancient oak pews, two small windows near the altar, which may be Norman, and a 15th-century rood screen.

Coleridge, Wordsworth, Byron and Southey in West Somerset

During the late 18th and early 10th centuries the therapeutic effect of wild landscapes such as Exmoor became a great attraction to the poets of the time. While staying in this area Coleridge wrote *The Rime of the Ancient Mariner* and when staying at an Exmoor farm on the coast of Somerset between Porlock and Lynton he wrote *Kubla Khan*.

The influence of the Exmoor landscape, the tiny church of Culbone on the steeply wooded slopes leading down to the sea and the wild cliffs of Exmoor can clearly be appreciated in *The Rime of the Ancient Mariner*. The ending of *Kubla Khan* was lost for ever to Coleridge's memory because a 'person from Porlock' called on business before he had finished writing it down.

Coleridge spent many days walking on Exmoor, sometimes accompanied by his brother-in-law Robert Southey. He was also friendly with Wordsworth, who lived for a time nearby on the Quantocks, and was an acquaintance of Byron, so there is a strong verbal tradition that Byron, too, was a visitor to Exmoor.

3 Lynmouth Harbour to Combe Martin

via Lynton and Martinhoe Roman Fortlet
13³/₄ miles (22.1 km)

Many of the buildings around the harbour at Lynmouth are new. On 15 August 1952, a cloudburst on Exmoor caused an unprecedented movement of boulders and tree trunks down to the riverbed in the village during the night, which led to a massive surge of water that washed away buildings and caused the death of thirty-four people.

There are three possibilities for walking up to the North Walk which takes you round the cliff to the Rocky Valley. All involve steep zig-zag paths, and turning right (west) at the top. One starts beside the Rising Sun, one near the cliff railway, and last of all, my favourite, a woodland path from near the end of the Esplanade, signed to Lynton, not far from the last turning circle. The cliff railway **15** was opened in 1880 and was partly

Castle Rock at Wringcliff Bay near Lynton. Wild goats often graze here, and round the corner is the famous Valley of Rocks.

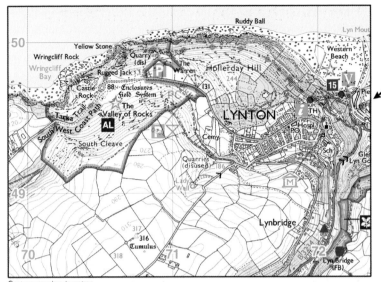

Contours are given in metres
The vertical interval is 10m

financed by local resident Sir George Newnes of the publishing company. It is driven by the weight of water in a tank of the downcoming car. When the car reaches the bottom, the water is emptied out and the car at the top has its tank filled until it starts its slow downward descent, pulling the other car to the top. If you do use the railway, turn left when you get to the street and next left again to get to the North Walk.

Having joined the North Walk, under water power or your own steam, so to speak, continue along it, around Hollerday Hill, to the Valley of Rocks. Below the rocks called Rugged Jack you may be fortunate enought to see mountain goats clinging to the cliff edge. Looking west across Lee Bay and Woody Bay, the headland in the distance is Highveer Point with the Cow and Calf headland a little nearer, and Wringapeak on the other side of Woody Bay.

Soon you round a corner and see ahead of you Wringcliff Bay with Castle Rock towering above it, and Duty Point Tower, a folly on the headland east of Lee Bay. Follow the road for about 100 yards past the roundabout and Castle Rock. Where you come in to full view of Wringcliff Bay, follow the higher path leading through the bracken to the seaward side of the road. Just before a stone wall the path turns steeply uphill and up stone steps to return to the road at the entrance to the Lee Abbey Estate.

47

Pass the Lee Abbey archway entrance to your right and continue straight on down the road into the valley below. At the bottom of the valley zig-zag up the road through the woods high above Lee Bay, until you are looking directly back at the Abbey. Leave the road down wooden steps and make for Crook Point.

Rejoin the road before going seawards into the woods 200 yards (180 metres) after the turning to Slattenslade.

The track crosses a small bridge over a tumbling stream into the woods. Soon after passing a house you come on to a surfaced road, officially a public bridleway, which you follow westwards. This track reaches a hairpin bend **A** towards the western end of Woody Bay. On the corner of the bend is a gate. Go through this and continue westwards along a forest track.

As you leave Woodybay Wood, ahead of you are the steep slopes leading up towards a Roman fortlet **16** (see page 56), and round the next corner you will see a magnificent waterfall, the sort you can stand under to get cool. This is Hollow Brook, which issues from a spring just above Martinhoe. In spring note the masses of ramsons (wild garlic). Looking back east you will now see the cave at Wringapeak which has pierced right through the headland, letting the sea surge through from both directions, to dramatic effect during stormy weather.

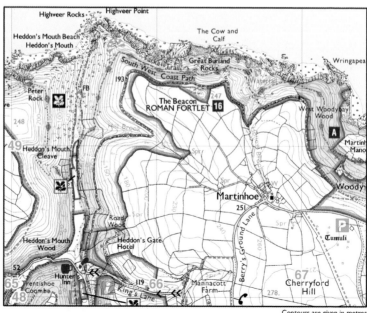

Contours are given in metres
The vertical interval is 10m

You will soon be looking down on the mouth of the River Heddon. The circular building you can see is one of the lime kilns, once supplied with coal and limestone shipped into Heddon's Mouth from South Wales.

The path now turns inland and downwards until it joins the Riverside Walk towards The Hunter's Inn. Just upstream from this point there is a stone bridge that you cross, briefly going downstream on the western side to join a track on the other side, then continuing upstream (left) again.

Look out for a path through the woodland next right, which rises back towards the coast. Continue to this direction until you come out of the woods and into a steep, dry valley covered in bracken, silver birch and hawthorn. Here the Coast Path zig-zags in wide sweeps until halfway up, at about 330 feet (100 metres), where it once again turns seawards right across the dry valley.

The narrow grassy path continues coastwards to Peter Rock overlooking the treacherous rocks at the mouth of the River Heddon. Continue west from Peter Rock on a well-made but narrow path that follows the very steep upper slopes of the cliffs. First keeping level and then rising, a distinctive slate-surfaced track just under a yard wide traverses heather-covered slopes with outcrops of jagged slate and some scree. After one more

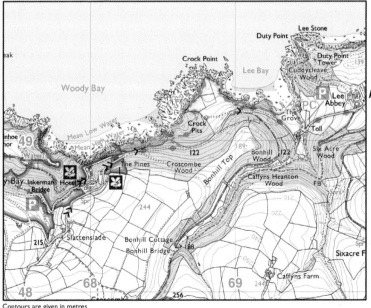

Contours are given in metres
The vertical interval is 10m

Looking towards the sea from the head of Heddon's Mouth Cleave.

steep rise around East Cleave a magnificent view of the cliffs to the west opens up. Here the path turns briefly south to reach the top of the coastal slopes and then follows the distinctive Devon stone and earth field boundary at the top of these clifftop slopes. At North Cleave Gut, after recent erosion, the path briefly goes though gates into the sheep grazed fields.

You will see Neck Wood clinging to the clifftop slopes just below you to the west and the heights of Trentishoe Down and Holdstone Down to the south-west, each around 1,000 feet (300 metres) high. You do not have to reach the top of either of them! Just before the deep gully east of Neck Wood, turn into the field through the gate and make your way round the back of the coastal hollows, by and large keeping your height as you do so. At the far western end you will find gates that let you out on to the unenclosed National Trust land. Follow the well-defined stony track due west, rising steadily until you come to a stone and earth boundary. Pass through the gap in the boundary and you may be able to see small circular humps, hollow in the middle, about 10–14 yards inland of the Coast Path. These are Bronze Age hut circles **17**, the dwellings of the inhabitants of Trentishoe some 3,000 years ago.

(If you are coming from the west, cross the field, making for the clifftop stile, then follow the field boundary on the cliff side until it turns abruptly inland. This is East Cleave and, by following the distinctive path on a ledge around the upper part of the steep slopes near Heddon's Mouth, you will soon reach Heddon's Mouth Cleave, the dry valley through which the path zig-zags down to the River Heddon. On reaching the river, go briefly downstream, cross the bridge, and join the footpath that rises steadily on the other side of Heddon's Mouth (eastern side). Then continue until you come out on to the lane to the Valley of Rocks. There, take the path towards the cliffs, keep going eastwards, and you will emerge near the head of the cliff railway at Lynton.)

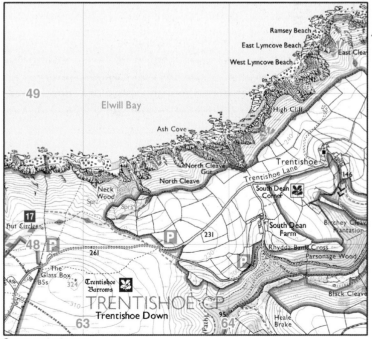

Contours are given in metres
The vertical interval is 10m

Trentishoe and Holdstone Downs, with the Great Hangman beyond.

You soon join a wide grassy track leading down from the coast road. Looking across the Bristol Channel, you are now due south of The Mumbles, with Swansea and Port Talbot steelworks to the right and the Gower Peninsula to the left.

The track begins to descend gently and passes through the centre of some partially improved sheep pasture, after which it arrives at a substantial stone and earth field boundary overlooking Sherrycombe. The Coast Path now goes inland until you will see a group of farm buildings, Holdstone Farm. Branch down at 45 degrees from the field boundary, still heading inland but gradually descending into the valley of Sherrycombe. Downhill and ahead you will see the National Trust sign for the 'Great Hangman'. Go through the gate and continue down towards the bridge over the stream. On the far side of the valley you will see the Coast Path rising steadily in a seaward direction across the western side of the combe.

(If you are coming from the west, take the diagonal path sloping down into Sherrycombe, go straight up the hill opposite, through the National Trust boundary, then keep left, seawards, gradually bearing round towards the east along the broad track mentioned above).

Travelling west, you will now approach the heights of Girt (Great) Down. Keep up the path until it comes close to a substantial field boundary corner. Turn left (west), keeping parallel to the cliffs. At the end of the wall, fork slightly seawards up a broad track going north-west. Make for a cairn ahead, which marks the summit of the Great Hangman, at 1,043 feet (318 metres) the highest point on the South West Coast Path. The name may have nothing to do with capital punishment or sheep stealing. *Hang* is the Saxon word for slope – the sloping hill – and the second part of the name relates to the Celtic word for hill (*mynedd*) as in the Old Man of Hoy or East Man and West Man in Purbeck. The pure Celtic base of the languages still spoken in Brittany, Ireland and Scotland bears no derivation from any other European language, having a common root only in Sanskrit. This is almost certainly why the Latin word for hill (*mons, montis*), bears similarities to the Celtic word *mynedd* (pronounced 'muneth') giving us two good reasons why a hill might end up with the name 'man'.

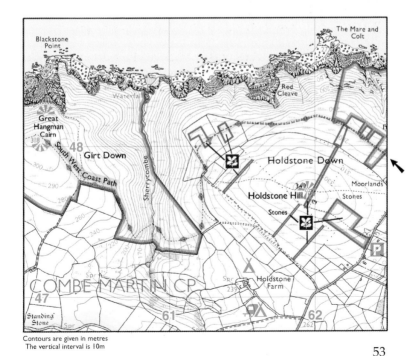

Contours are given in metres
The vertical interval is 10m

Ahead of you lies Combe Martin Bay with the pyramidal shape of Little Hangman in the foreground. Go straight on towards Little Hangman, following the ridge and then follow the fence on the seaward side. Go down some wooden steps, still keeping outside the fields and at the top of the cliff slopes. Just before you reach the Little Hangman the Coast Path goes left and below the inland side of the Little Hangman until it directly overlooks Combe Martin Bay. Now follow the clifftop slopes, keeping outside the fence around the back of Wild Pear Beach.

The Coast Path continues along the top of the cliff, and views of Combe Martin Church soon open up. In spring, herb Robert, campion, ground ivy, bluebells, primroses, violets, foxgloves, celandines and wood sage line the clifftop path, which soon rises to look back at the Little Hangman with the moorland top of Great (or Big) Hangman on the horizon. This is Lester Cliff. Continue westwards to a rain shelter next to the NT sign for the Little Hangman. Just past the rain shelter the official route goes inland left into Combe Martin behind a row of houses. If you choose to follow the cliff top there is a very steep path through the bushes and across the lawns with nice views of the old harbour. Little can be detected of the small fishing settlement that must once have been associated with this fine natural harbour. Combe Martin is now predominantly an Edwardian village and apart from the ugly clifftop caravans, which are mainly visible only from the Coast Path, it is now a quiet and pleasant resort.

One small piece of evidence of a former trade with South Wales is the name of the car park – the Kiln car park.

The mines of Combe Martin

There is a legend that there was a trade in silver and lead from the Combe Martin mines to the Mediterranean by visiting Phoenician merchants, and we know that the mines were in full operation in the late 13th century. The silver probably enabled the English to pay for their escapades in France, at Crecy, Poitiers and Agincourt. The mines closed 150 years ago.

Combe Martin Bay

Combe Martin Bay

Scotch Stone
Hangman Point

Rawn's
Rocks

Blackstone
Beach

Little Hangman

MLW

Spr

48

Wild Pear
Beach

North
Challacombe

East
Challacombe

Spr

Lester Cliff

119

West
Challacombe

Girt Farm

Sch

38

Netherton Cross

156

Knap Down

47

Furze
Park

Silver Dale
Nurseries

232

PO

Silver Mines
Farm

Mines
(dis)

West Park
Farm

Spr

Combe Martin

TH
26

Corners

Clorridge
Hill

146

Quarry
(disused)
Cave

Skirhead
Farm

132

46

102

The Rectory

146

BS
Hotel

68

Brimball
Hill

Hodges
Wood

Lower
Hodges

Quarries
(dis)

Quarries
(dis)

Higher
Hodges
Farm

Ridge Hill

Rectory
Wood

Spr

MS

248

Stoneditch
Hill

W

Withycombe

45

Yetland
Farm

212

Henstridge

Quarry
(dis)

Yellaton

Wheel
Cross

Wheel Farm

Henstridge Wood

Indicknowle Wood

Yellaton
Wood

Yellaton Lane

Thornlands

Thornland
Wood

Brinscott
Wood

Indicknowle

188

58

59

Contours are given in metres
The vertical interval is 10m

55

A CIRCULAR WALK TO MARTINHOE ROMAN FORTLET

5 miles (8 km)

From The Hunter's Inn (National Trust car park, grid ref. SS655 482) go right (east) of the pub following the upper route towards the sea. This path rises gradually, branching east round a steep valley, and continues north-west to join the crest of the clifftop slopes going east. Look back at the rocky outcrop of Lundy (seemingly joined to land from this viewpoint). Round the corner, a small stony path zig-zags up towards steps through a stone wall to the Martinhoe Roman fortlet **16**, at just under 800 feet (245 metres). Here you will see a series of concentric low earth banks, and excavations revealed two blocks of barrack buildings for about 80 Roman soldiers. The lookout was built to keep an eye on the inhabitants of Wales, the Silures, around AD 59.

To continue the circular walk, retrace your steps and follow the track east until you come to West Woodybay Wood, where it turns south to follow the edge of the wood. After 545 yards (500 metres) you will come to a junction where you turn left and seawards to join the Coast Path. Follow this route west past the waterfall to Heddon's Mouth. Follow the Coast Path inland to a bridge over the River Heddon. Here continue upstream to reach The Hunter's Inn again.

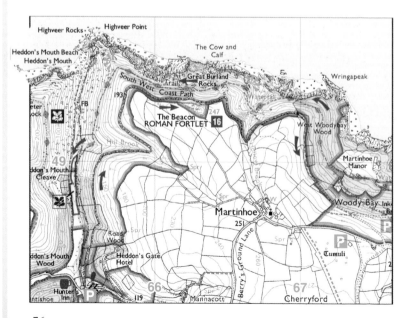

The coast at Martinhoe, looking east across Woody Bay and Lee Bay to The Foreland at Countisbury.

4 Combe Martin to Mortehoe and Woolacombe, including Lundy Island

13 miles (20.8 km)

Follow the coast road west up the hill and around the corner above the beach. Just before the main road straightens out, a tarmac lane leads seawards. Go along it, past the former parish boundary marker between Combe Martin and Berrynarbor, and sharp right up a sunken lane. This lane rejoins the main road **A** to follow the footway that runs parallel with it. In due course the footway returns to the old road. Turn left and then right to follow the new A399 coastal road west for about 400 yards (365 metres) until you reach the crest of a hill opposite the signed turning for Berrynarbor. A Coast Path sign on your right takes you on to a quiet lane leading north to the Sandycove Hotel. Keeping just to the landward side of the hotel follow the old coast road north-westwards until you see a drive entering from the landward side. Just before this leave the track to go seawards through a gate and down wooden steps. Soon you are looking into a little cove with high cliffs around it and a small fulmar colony.

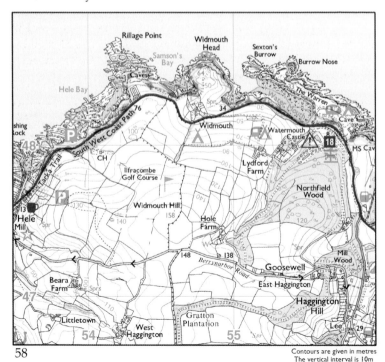

Contours are given in metres
The vertical interval is 10m

The Coast Path follows the seaward side of the camping fields and then turns inland to the main road after crossing a stone arched bridge over a swift stream. Turn right along a narrow fenced path parallel with the main road. When it rejoins the road keep on past the car park and caravan site/main harbour vehicle entrance to a gate into Water Mouth itself. Watermouth Castle **18**, was built in Gothic style in 1825 and is now an entertainment centre.

Normally you should be able to follow the edge of Water Mouth but, at high tide, you may have to follow the road west and take the stile into the wood to rejoin the Coast Path. Be extremely careful if you do this as there is currently no provision for pedestrians; there are plans to remedy this.

As the path leaves the woods keep to the seaward side of the meadow. The headland is Widmouth Head and you are soon below the old coastguard lookout with a view of Lundy due west above Rillage Point, the coast of Wales to the north, and the rugged cliffs of Exmoor to the east. In Samson's Bay more fulmars glide around their nesting area on the cliffs.

Turn right (west) sharply as you come within sight of Widmouth Farm. Keep on along the cliff top to Rillage Point. From here you can see Ilfracombe just 1 mile (2 km) ahead. From Rillage Point the Coast Path returns to run alongside the coast road, partly on a separate path and partly on the verge, until it reaches a picnic area. Follow the pavement down into Hele, turn right (seawards) at the Hele Bay Hotel, go down to the beach, and then up the steps to the seaward side of the toilets.

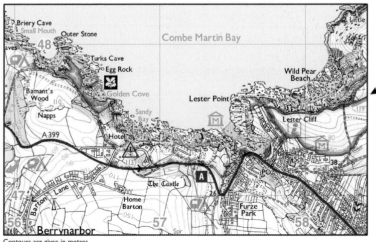

Contours are given in metres
The vertical interval is 10m

Sunset behind Lantern Hill and St Nicholas Chapel, Ilfracombe.

Zig-zag up the hill, observing any diversion signs necessitated by recent cliff-falls. Nearly at the top you will see some iron railings, from where there is a fine view over Ilfracombe and Lundy Island. The Coast Path now returns inland for 100 yards or so, and turns westwards again as you come once more into full view of Ilfracombe. The massive ramparts here are the remains of the double-banked Iron Age promontory fort of Hillsborough. Make your way into the town to explore the harbour and visit the lifeboat house and St Nicholas Chapel **19** and lighthouse. Town trail leaflets are available from the Tourist Information Centre.

On entering Ilfracombe Harbour, look for the blue street tile signs to guide you through the town. To leave the harbour turn left into Hierns Lane and then right into Broad Street. Continue towards the quay for 150 yards, then turn left into Capstone Road keeping the public house on your right.

At the end of Capstone Road turn right along Capstone Parade. On reaching Wildersmouth Beach, aim for the New Landmark Theatre. Take the steps up round the seaward side of this building and follow the path up through the gardens and out through a silver metal garden gate on to Granville Road. Turn right and follow this road until you reach a turning on your right which is Torrs Walk Avenue. (This is the quieter end of Ilfracombe and if you continue down Granville Road and up Torrs Park there are several accommodation opportunities.) Where Torrs Walk Avenue forks, go right between the white garden wall, nearly to the cliff top and

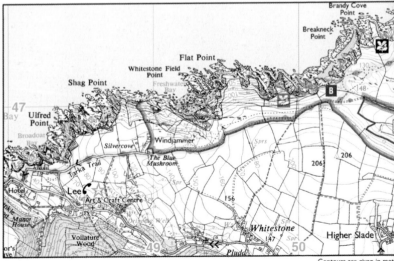

then left through the bushes. Twenty yards (18 metres) west of this, go seawards from the National Trust sign for a 220-yard (200-metre) walk along the cliff edge, before zig-zagging up the Seven Hills southwards, going right (west) at a junction on the way up.

Bull Point and the top of the lighthouse have just come into sight to the west with Lundy in the background. When you reach the top, Seven Hills, go left and a few yards inland and right to join the clearly defined grass track west, which goes to the seaward side of the highest rocky outcrops. Just before **B**, turn inland and then once again westwards to follow what is now a farm track but used to be the old coast road from Ilfracombe to Lee.

Keep to the farm track west until, near some bungalows, it becomes a lane which takes you all the way to Lee. Once there, follow the road round the back of the beach and west up the hill.

(If you are coming from the west, take the road round the back of the beach and go behind the Lee Bay Hotel. At the back of the hotel building you will see a steep lane rising left (east) – this is the Coast Path to Ilfracombe.)

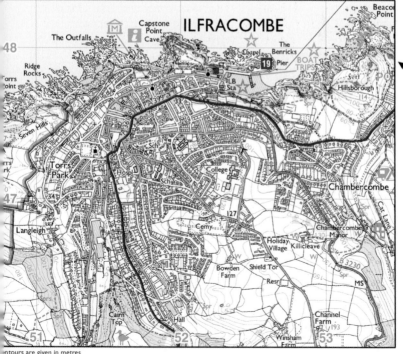

ntours are given in metres
he vertical interval is 10m

Going west from Lee Bay, climb up the road until you come to a National Trust sign for Damage Cliffs. Go through the wicket-gate, right (west), and follow the cliff top. The prehistoric standing stones **20** shown on the map are likely to have been religious monuments during the Early Bronze Age.

Between here and Bull Point **21** the path dips to sea level and twice rises again to over 200 feet (60 metres). The path is well defined and provided with steps in the steeper places. When you see the lighthouse at Bull Point, first constructed in 1879, make for the landward side of the lighthouse enclosure, follow it, and cross the lighthouse road to continue south-west close to the cliff top. The path crosses a grassy area to a flight of steps up some small cliffs, after which it continues, for 1¼ miles (2 km), all the way along the cliff top to Morte Point.

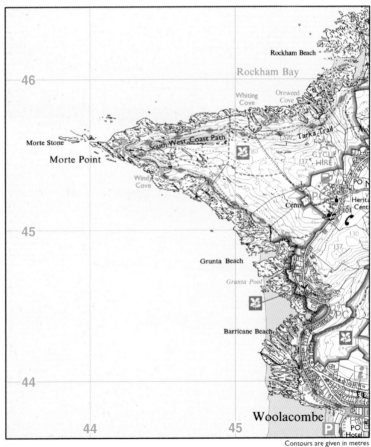

Contours are given in metres
The vertical interval is 10m

On the way, you must wind in and out among little knolls before dropping down to Rockham Beach, where you may see your first seal. You may also hear the rattling noise of the tiny whitethroat and see it hopping among the gorse bushes.

After passing Whiting Cove, the Coast Path rises briefly to a seat, before descending again westwards to follow the lower part of the cliff slopes towards Morte Point. As you round Morte Point heading for Woolacombe, the coast of Wales disappears and a new view opens up of virtually the whole of the rest of the North Devon coast. In the foreground is the wide sweep of Woolacombe Sand and Morte Bay with Baggy Point in the middle distance. Mortehoe and Woolacombe have pleasant accommodation, and Mortehoe Church, of Norman origin, has some interesting features, including medieval bench-ends.

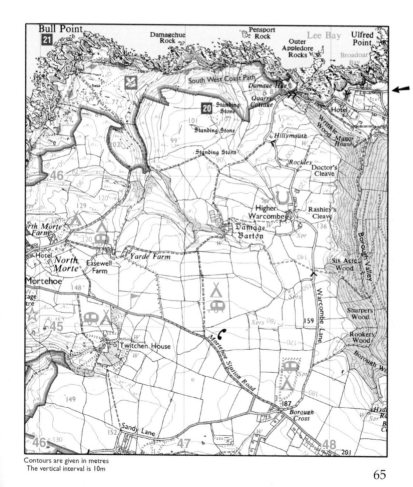

Contours are given in metres
The vertical interval is 10m

A Circular Walk on Lundy Island

4¹/₂ miles (7.4 km) or 7 miles (11 km)

If you study the timetables you may manage to spend all day on Lundy and do a complete circuit of the island. From the landing pier head up the road to the Marisco Tavern, which may be serving meals, including breakfast. In the nearby shop you can buy guidebooks, maps and food, and there is an information point. Return past the church of St Helena, built in the 1800s by the Rev. Heaven. Keep along the southern cliff top to the Marisco Castle, originally built for Henry III in 1240 but now holiday accommodation. Here you have a dramatic view of the southern lighthouse, built on a slate promontory which juts out from this granite island, protecting the harbour below.

From the castle turn west to follow the 400-foot (124-metre) cliffs until you come to the old lighthouse. It was abandoned because low cloud or sea fog rendered it too often ineffective. Now head north along the cliff top on the high, flat plateau of the island to Battery Point. Look out for the top end of a well-built granite wall which runs down sea- wards just below and behind a rocky clifftop outcrop. This indicates the narrow path from the cliff top down to a ruined cottage and cannon emplacement which gave this headland its name.

If you are short of time turn inland to the man-made Pondsbury Pond, head north-east and then turn right (south) over the brow and down on to the track along the eastern undercliff of the island. The track was once a railway built to carry the granite which was used all over the Empire. Seals are often visible and there is a rich marine wildlife. Unpolluted, sheltered and fed by the Atlantic and the Gulf Stream, the waters here were designated as Britain's first statutory marine nature reserve. Sika deer graze the undercliff. Be sure you know all about Lyme Disease before wandering in the undergrowth (see page 38).

If you have time continue to do the full round walk keep north along the cliffs. At Threequarters Wall, looking back along the cliffs, with a powerful enough telescope, you may sight Lundy's own rare puffins, all that is left of a massive colony. With sturdy boots you could explore the eastern undercliff paths and on the top you can walk anywhere you like across the short springy turf provided by the grazing goats, sheep and rabbits. At the end of either walk make for the Marisco Tavern and prepare to return down to the pier.

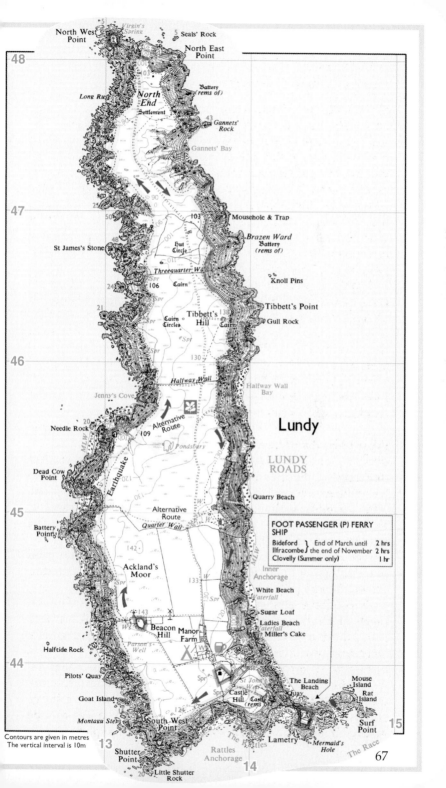

Lundy

LUNDY
ROADS

Contours are given in metres
The vertical interval is 10m

North West Point
Virgin's Spring
Seals' Rock
North East Point
Battery (rems of)
Long Rus
North End
Settlement
Gannets' Rock
Gannets' Bay
Mousehole & Trap
St James's Stone
Hut Circle
Brazen Ward Battery (rems of)
Threequarter Wall
Knoll Pins
Cairn
Cairn Circles
Tibbett's Hill
Cairn
Tibbett's Point
Gull Rock
Halfway Wall
Halfway Wall Bay
Jenny's Cove
Needle Rock
Alternative Route
Pondsbury
Dead Cow Point
Earthquake
Quarry Beach
Alternative Route
Quarter Wall
FOOT PASSENGER (P) FERRY SHIP
Bideford } End of March until 2 hrs
Ilfracombe } the end of November 2 hrs
Clovelly (Summer only) 1 hr
Battery Point
Ackland's Moor
Inner Anchorage
White Beach
Waterfall
Sugar Loaf
Ladies Beach
Waterfall
Miller's Cake
Beacon Hill
Manor Farm
Parson's Well
Halftide Rock
Pilots' Quay
St John's Well
The Landing Beach
Quay
Mouse Island
Rat Island
Goat Island
Castle Hill
Castle (rems of)
Montagu Steps
South-West Point
Surf Point
Shutter Point
Lamerty
Mermaid's Hole
The Rattles
Rattles Anchorage
Little Shutter Rock
The Race

The landing beach and southern lighthouse on Lundy Island.

Lundy Island

This 3-mile- (5-km)-long island, whose name derives from the Norse for puffin, can often be visited for the day from Ilfracombe or Bideford. Consult the timetables available from a local Tourist Information Centre or on the website www.lundyisland.co.uk (for accommodation or camping book well ahead). Since 1969 the island has been owned by the National Trust who have leased it to the Landmark Trust. The sailing schedules are based on tides, as is the amount of time that day visitors have to explore. The puffins, razorbills and guillemots are normally in residence only from April until late June or early July.

You will land on the pier at the south of the island (see page 66 for a circular walk). There are the ruins of Marisco Castle, the old lighthouse, and 7 miles (11.25 km) of superb rugged coast-line, including 400-foot (120-metre) cliffs, with views of the coasts of Devon (of which Lundy is officially part), Cornwall, Pembrokeshire and Glamorgan. The whole top of the island is a flat plateau, with tracks, paths across the short springy turf and open access. There are more challenging cliff-edge paths for those appropriately shod and seeking something more adventurous. A stay of several days would be even better than a day trip but you would have to organise it well in advance. The accommodation varies from fishermen's huts to castles!

5 Mortehoe and Woolacombe to Braunton

around Baggy Point
15 miles (24.1 km) from Woolacombe

As you approach the centre of Woolacombe from Mortehoe and see a car park and phone boxes on your right, take the road going right (west) and follow it, leaving the beach access to your right (unless you plan to walk across the sands to Putsborough). Ignore any small paths that lead into the sand dunes on the right and continue to a bridleway sign with the Coast Path pointing right along a short stretch of tarmac. The original official Coast Path then keeps in the dunes until the far end of the NT property, where it rises up a ridge and joins the Marine Drive via another steep set of steps as it becomes a narrower bridleway, then a well-defined track on the ridge above the settlement of Vention. Look across at the Baggy Point peninsula, so that you can work out your route to Baggy Point along the top of the cliff slopes.

(If you have strong feelings about eroding the coastal dune system, or don't want to walk on soft sand for the next kilometre, just continue within the flat grassy area behind the dunes for a while. Then, by the beach access at **A**, branch slightly uphill and inland along a wide grassy path. When you come to a fork where a path descends into the lower dunes at **B**, you can continue uphill and then left to join the Marine Drive by a steep flight of steps.)

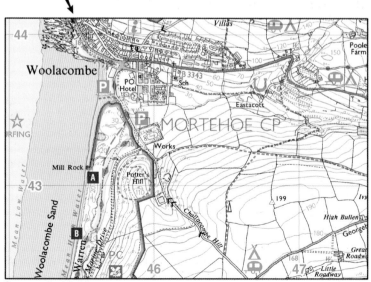

Contours are given in metres
The vertical interval is 10m

Either way the Coast Path at Vention then emerges on to the county road. Keep straight ahead along the road for about 200 yards (180 metres), and then turn right (west) at the crest of the hill through a 7-bar steel gate with a stile beside it. Follow the track ahead beside the field boundary until you reach the top of the steeper slope and then branch about 20 degrees to the right until you come to the gorse-covered clifftop slopes. The Coast Path stays at the top of these slopes, meandering in and out of the gorse in places.

From Baggy Point you can enjoy one of the closest mainland views of Lundy Island (see pages 66 and 68). Looking almost due north across the rocks off Morte Point you may see Swansea and the Gower Peninsula. With good binoculars and on a very clear day, you will be able to make out the smoking chimneys of the Milford Haven oil refineries and the cliffs of Pembrokeshire.

Contours are given in metres
The vertical interval is 10m

From the southern side of Baggy Point you can see what lies ahead on the route, with Bideford Bay in the foreground. From Westward Ho! to Hartland Point, where you may see the lighthouse flashing, is all unspoilt coastline. Halfway along you may be able to identify Buck's Mills nestling in a small combe beside the sea and, slightly to the right of centre, Clovelly. The Coast Path stays more or less on the cliff top for the whole of that stretch.

To continue, go to the far, south-west, corner of Baggy Point, and follow the yard-wide stone path that starts down the cliff towards the point and then turns sharply back towards Croyde Bay (see page 72) to continue on the level along the coastal slope.

Keep straight on down this path, which becomes the village street. Continue past the National Trust car park and along the lane until you see a sign to the beach opposite a bus shelter.

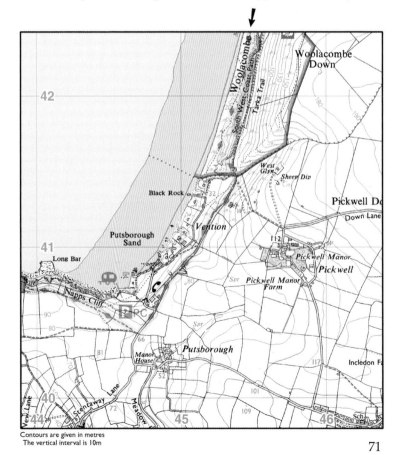

Contours are given in metres
The vertical interval is 10m

Contours are given in met
The vertical interval is 10

Turn right (south) down the lane and make your way on to the sandy beach and towards the far southern corner. The official route goes along the base of the dunes over a bridge, but I found it easier to keep to the hard sand by the water.

At the southernmost end you will see a flight of steps leaving the beach: these are private. Make for the nearby wartime blockhouse and turn right **C** (west), walking along a line of rocks just under the cliff. Continue under the cliff round the corner across one tiny sandy beach, and the path climbs to the cliff top via another flight of steps. Turn right to continue along the low grassy cliff until Saunton Sands come into sight. Make for the old coastguard lookout above you, where you have to cross the main road by turning left and then right to rejoin the path, which rises up some concrete steps before turning right (south), and continues above and parallel to the main coast road.

Before you descend to the main road at the Saunton Sands Hotel, look south at the Braunton Burrows sand dunes, a major part of the Biosphere Reserve. On the main road there is a bus stop **D** for the Croyde–Saunton–Barnstaple buses, which you may wish to take if river estuaries and sand dunes do not appeal as much as the rugged cliffs. As you approach the main road, you have a choice. The official route loops round the landward side of the Saunton Sands Hotel and follows a track south of the houses on the coast road. It then joins the main road for 330 yards (300 metres) to Saunton, taking the first turning right after the golf course entrance. A more attractive alternative footpath, with fine views over Braunton Burrows and the Taw and Torridge Estuary, has been provided over Saunton Down which avoids a road section. For this, as you approach the main road, turn left inland away from it and up a steep zig-zag to the top of the hill. At the top turn along the ridge and go down the hill towards Braunton. Follow the track across the fields and down into a valley and

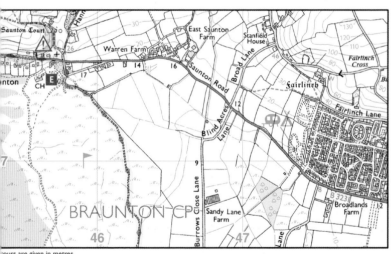

cours are given in metres
vertical interval is 10m

carry on to the right of Saunton Court where it becomes a sur-faced road; keep right and go straight on at the crossroads.

Where the lane turns sharp left, carry straight on through a wicket-gate **E**, across the field, and through a bridlegate, which takes you on to the golf course. Turn left (south-east) down the broad sandy bridleway jeep track past a red-tiled barn and keep to this sandy track as it continues south. When you come into sight of Braunton on your left and the track becomes less well defined, bear briefly left onto a grassy track, and then continue south keeping close to a windswept thicket separating the path from a field on the landward side. The path continues in the same general direction through thickets, winding its way southwards.

Braunton Burrows are used by the Ministry of Defence for training with live firing taking place on 30 days a year. However, the Coast Path goes around the edge of the range, and so can still be used even when the Red Warning flags are flying.

Carry straight on south until reaching a T-junction with a stone track **F**. Turn left (inland) and you will come in a few yards to a car park with an information board. The boundaries of both the Nature Reserve and the Army Danger Area are indicated on the maps.

When you reach a parking area **G** at the end of the track you can follow a board walk west, still through sand dunes, to look at the mouth of the River Taw, before retracing your steps to the car park. The Coast Path continues east along another broad stone track with low marshy meadows on the left and bramble-covered dunes on the right.

Looking across the Taw and Torridge Estuaries to Appledore from Braunton Burrows Nature Reserve.

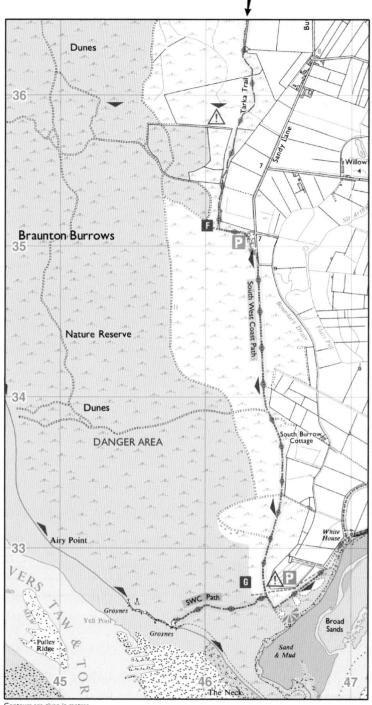

Dunes

Tarka Trail

Sandy Lane

Willow

7

Braunton Burrows

F

P 7

South West Coast Path

Boundary Drain

Flat Pill

Nature Reserve

Dunes

DANGER AREA

South Burrow
Cottage

Airy Point

White
House

G

P

VERS TAW & TOR

Grosnes

Yelland Pool

Groynes

SWC Path

Broad
Sands

Pulley
Ridge

Sand
& Mud

The Neck

Contours are given in metres
The vertical interval is 10m

Banks of the River Taw Estuary at the White House, Braunton Burrows.

You soon come to White House. Here the track becomes a surfaced toll road heading north, and the Coast Path turns right and then left along the dyke beside the estuary all the way to Braunton, 2^1/$_2$ miles (4 km) away. As you approach the village the river widens. This is Velator Quay, once busy with boats bringing limestone and coal from across the Bristol Channel, with five smoking lime kilns producing slaked lime during the early 19th century. Now you will see recreation boats moored instead.

When the riverside walk finishes, cross the sluice and take the road past an industrial estate to a (new) roundabout. Turn right onto the gated and tarmaced track of the old Ilfracombe–Barnstaple Railway, which is now the Coast Path.

Braunton's 13th-century church is worth a visit. The village can be reached along the former railway by turning left and forking right (north) at the roundabout **H**. The Braunton Countryside Centre has exhibitions about the area's attractions, such as the Great Field, and there is a Tourist Information Centre. Braunton Great Field, 350 acres (142 hectares) of medieval open-field system, is still in cultivation in the traditional fashion.

The Barnstaple to Ilfracombe Railway

The Coast Path from Braunton to Barnstaple, which is also the Tarka Trail Cycleway, is the former Barnstaple to Ilfracombe Railway. In 1870, the Barnstaple and Ilfracombe Railway Company obtained permission to build the line. Four years later it was completed despite the challenges presented by the steep hills and valleys. The line was originally single track, then doubled and finally became a single line before closure.

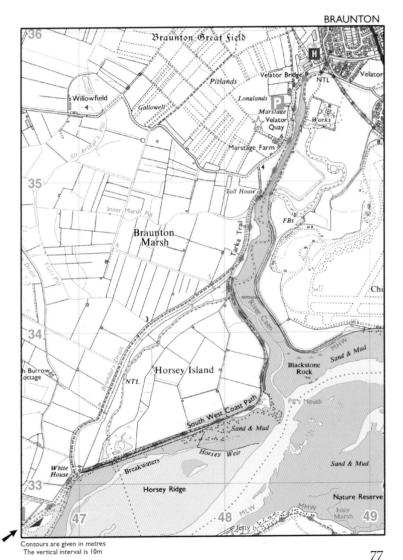

Contours are given in metres
The vertical interval is 10m

6 Braunton to Westward Ho!

via Bideford and Appledore
23³/₄ miles (38.2 km)

From Braunton, if you are starting a section of the walk here, go down South Street or the old railway line south and continue until you see the roundabout **H**. Continue past Signal Court on your right before you join the Tarka Trail and walk for 5 miles (8 km) to Barnstaple up one side of the estuary. After that you will go the same distance back down the other side to Instow, where there is sometimes a ferry to Appledore in high season either side of high tides. Unless you choose to shorten your walk by taking the ferry, continue a further 3 miles (5 km) up the Torridge Estuary to Bideford Bridge and back down the estuary to Appledore. Depending on the time of year you may see egret, oyster catcher and curlew right beside the railway embankment. Make sure you have your binoculars and a good bird book with you.

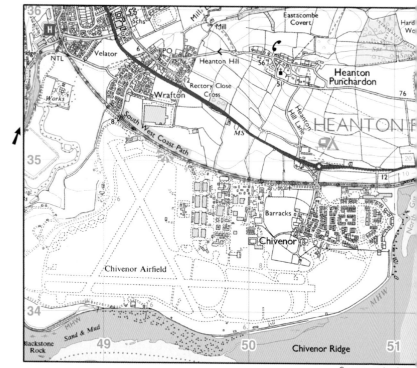

Contours are given in met
The vertical interval is 10

Riverside walk and the 15th-century bridge at Barnstaple.

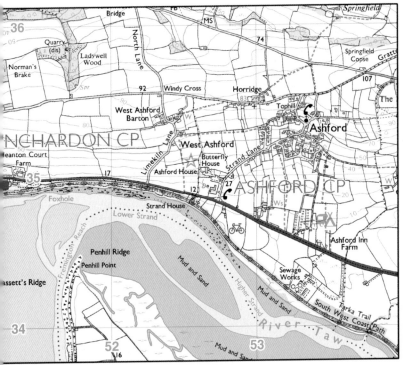

Contours are given in metres
The vertical interval is 10m

As you approach Barnstaple you will see the new downstream bridge which incorporates a cycle route and an alternative route of the Coast Path.

To go into Barnstaple, well worth the extra half mile, go over a swing bridge and along the Quay. There are lots of things to see in the town, plenty of pubs and shops and quite a lively scene, with the Pannier Market still used for markets on Tuesdays and Fridays.

To rejoin the Coast Path west, cross the 15th-century Long Bridge. There are industrial buildings on your right. To the landward side of them, beside their vehicle entrance, is a narrow footpath leading down to the peaceful riverbank path which then turns left to pass under the southernmost arch of the new bridge before rejoining the Coast Path on the trackbed of the former railway. The official route, however, follows a tarmac path which branches off the approach road and curves right below and close to the embankments of this (rather noisy) new road, and goes left under the bridge approach roads through a subway. At the far end of the subway it turns left again (joining a loop path which comes down from the bridge for those using the alternative route), and joins the former railway line just inland.

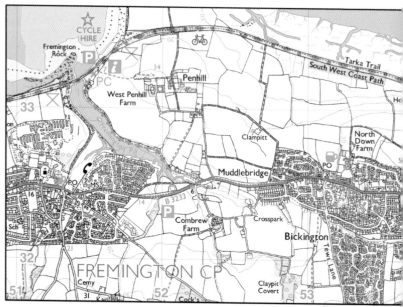

Contours are given in metre
The vertical interval is 10m

After 2½ miles (4 km) you will see Fremington Quay adjoining the railway line. Here they have rebuilt some railway platforms with a station building and signal box/lookout which you can get into through the café/heritage centre when it is open. The lookout gives good views across the river. The displays, illustrated with lots of fine old photos, explain the industrial archaeology of the Quay, a major staging point for Devon clay to be transferred from rail to boat and exported all over the world. Now you may still see ships from faraway parts tied up at Bideford Quay and being loaded with clay from road trucks.

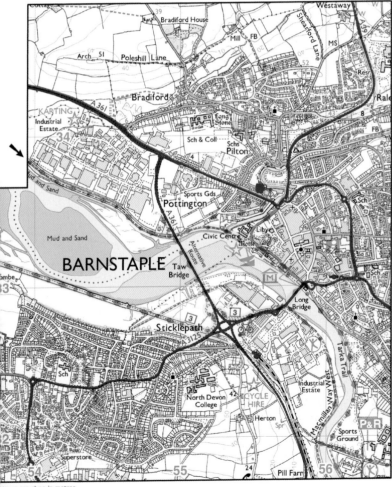

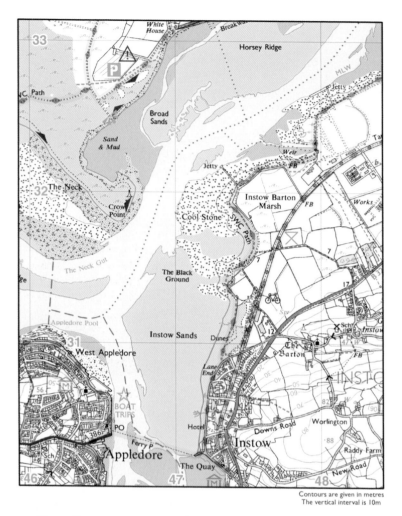

Contours are given in metres
The vertical interval is 10m

From Fremington Quay, the Coast Path continues along the Tarka Trail for about 1½ miles (2.5 km) to East Yelland Marsh, where you turn right, off the Tarka Trail, to follow a dyke by the River Taw. The dyke and the two large jetties you pass were constructed for the Yelland Power Station, which was demolished a few years ago, and natural vegetation is now being restored to the site. From that dyke you get great views across to Braunton Burrows and up both estuaries. In winter months it is also a good spot to watch birds feeding on the mudflats.

At the end of the dyke take the path leading onwards through the sand dunes until you come to a fingerpost marking a path junction. At low tide you can take a set of stone steps

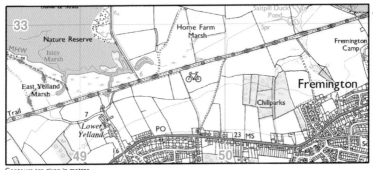

Contours are given in metres
The vertical interval is 10m

down on to the foreshore to continue around the headland to Instow Sands. Take care on this section as the rocks can be slippery. At high tide take the path leading inland along a track around the back of the cricket ground, and down a military road to rejoin the main route on Instow Sands. From here walk along the beach into the village of Instow, which has a good selection of shops, accommodation and places to eat.

In high season, subject to tides, it is possible to catch a ferry from Instow pier across to Appledore (although you will miss much of the estuary and the historic town of Bideford if you do). Assuming you are continuing on to Bideford, turn right at the old railway signal box 200 yards (180 metres) past the pier to join the Tarka Trail, which you follow through to Bideford Station.

The view from the Tarka Trail (part of the old Barnstaple–Bideford Railway).

The Tarka Trail and the National Cycle Network

The Coast Path from Lynton to Bideford coincides with the Tarka Trail. The 180-mile (300-km) trail makes use of part of the former Bideford–Okehampton Railway, following Tarka the otter's journeys along the River Torridge, with a southern link into Dartmoor and a return to Barnstaple down the Taw Valley. Bideford Station now has some old rolling stock, a small Tarka Trail Visitor Centre and a café in a 1950s railway carriage.

The Tarka Trail is part of the 100-mile Devon Coast to Coast National Cycleway (NN27) from Ilfracombe to Plymouth. From northern Devon it goes through Okehampton and Tavistock and skirts around the beautiful western slopes of Dartmoor (with another nearby railway line mountain bike detour to Princetown), past Saltram House (NT) and into Plymouth. It follows country lanes and old railway lines at both ends. There is a cycle-hire depot just below, and south of, Bideford station.

At Bideford, leave the railway and cross the ancient bridge across the River Torridge, then turn right (north) along Bideford Quay. Keep as close to the river as you can, going straight ahead at the small roundabout on the new housing estate to go under the high A39 bridge. Keep straight ahead past a cottage and alongside a high stone wall before turning back to the river along a narrow stone-wall-bordered passage. At the river's edge turn left (north) along the top of a low cliff. This takes you in front of a pleasant group of Victorian-style villas and past an old quay **A**.

When you see an array of 'private' and house-name signs in front of you **B**, take the middle path, which branches away from the river. Cross the valley past a small well and then go up the hill between tank traps, before turning back towards the river and the riverside National Trust property of Burrough Farm.

Keep to the riverside past the house at **C** and follow the substantial new dyke beside the estuary as far as the boatbuilders yard boundary. Follow the boundary, which runs directly inland at right angles to the river bank and curves right between hedges to emerge on a house drive. Turn left up this drive for a short distance and then right into a field just before another house. Go more or less due north across the small valley and upthe otherside of it onto the road into Appledore near a row of houses on the other side of the road. Go right down the road past the boatyard entrance into Appledore. *If you have any doubts about the state of the tide or the flow of water alongside the dyke, use the signed inland alternative.*

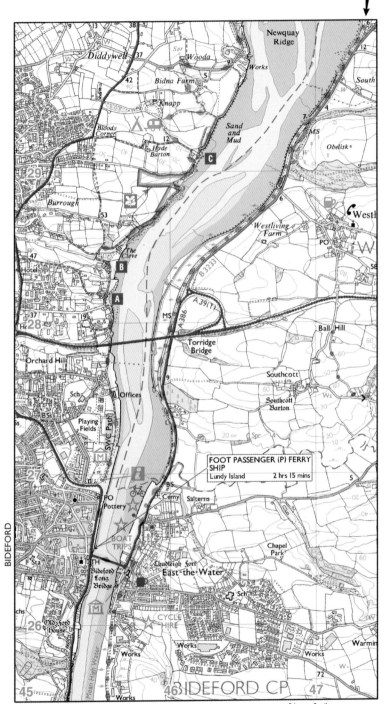

FOOT PASSENGER (P) FERRY SHIP
Lundy Island   2 hrs 15 mins

BIDEFORD

8 km or 5 miles   Contours are given in metres   5 km or 3 miles
A386 Great Torrington   The vertical interval is 10m   A65 Kendal

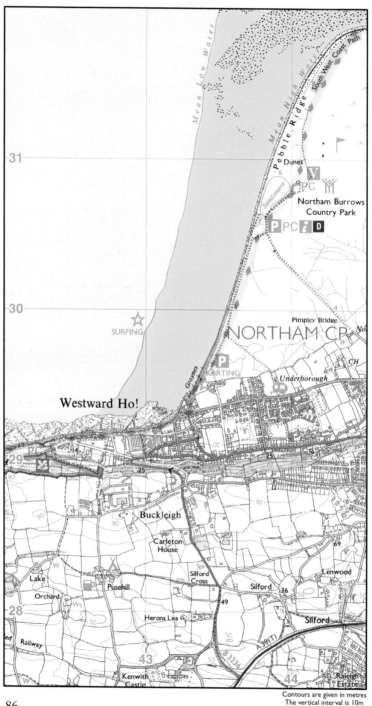

Mean Low Water

Mean High Water

Pebble Ridge

South West Coast Path

Dunes

Sandymere

V
PC

Northam Burrows
Country Park

P PC i D

30

Pimpley Bridge

SURFING

NORTHAM C.P.

No

CH

Groynes

KARTING

Underborough

Westward Ho!

14

29

25

80

90

Buckleigh

90

Carleton
House

69

Spr

Silford
Cross

Lenwood

Lake

W

Pusehill

Silford

36

50

Orchard

Ws

28

50

49

Herons Lea

Silford

Railway

50

A 39(T)

50

B 3236

60

43

44

Kenwith
Castle

Raleigh
Estate

W

Contours are given in metres
The vertical interval is 10m

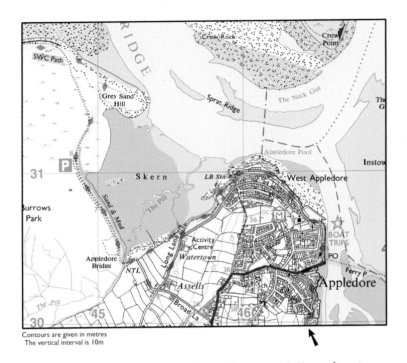

Contours are given in metres
The vertical interval is 10m

To continue towards Northam Burrows, follow the river-side road (Hubbastone Road) until you come to a T-junction. Turn right towards the river, which you now follow around West Appledore. After the lifeboat station keep to the path along the low cliff top. Just before the garage, at low tide, keep to the beach as far as the Country Park. The garage was formerly a boat-building hangar. If high tide forces you to use the road, turn along the road signposted for Northam Burrows Country Park. You make for the dunes ahead of you and, to your right, look across the estuary and Bideford Bar. You are now just 900 yards (825 metres) across the water from the dunes at Braunton Burrows.

The Coast Path now keeps close to the beach around the northern end of Northam Burrows before going inland of the fencing and posts which have been put up to protect the dunes until it comes to the information centre **D**, where there are toilets and a water tap. Keep just to the landward side of Sandymere and then along the back of the pebble ridge to Westward Ho!

Maritime enterprise in the Bristol Channel

Under Queen Elizabeth I, naval and trading activities were raised to an all-time height. At Minehead and Boscastle, old piers were given a new lease of life and at Buck's Mills, Clovelly and Hartland Quay, completely new harbours were created by the construction of piers, at enormous expense to the lords of the manors concerned. Hartland Quay, the remains of which you may see later in this walk, gained Parliamentary approval in the latter half of the 16th century and was certainly in full action by the beginning of the 17th century.

Ilfracombe Harbour and Lantern Hill – the departure point for Lundy.

The owner of Clovelly Court, George Carey, built the pier at Clovelly shortly before the end of the 16th century. The first reference to this pier is in 1597 when a labourer was paid 7d for bringing lime from Clovelly Quay to Stoke for use in the construction of the church.

These smaller quays were used mainly for local products being shipped in small quantities either from harbours on the Welsh coast or from neighbouring harbours, such a Bristol, Gloucester, Bideford and Barnstaple.

For example, in the middle of the 19th century, a small boat called the *Susanna* went from Hartland to Swansea and Newport to load coal, and made six trips to Caldy, Lydstep and Aberthaw to load limestone. It then went to Port Gaverne to fetch slate for building work from Delabole Quarries, while trips were also made to Barnstaple and Gloucester, quite possibly carrying farm produce from around Hartland. Occasionally, such a small boat would make a trip round Land's End in the spring if the weather was calm. Records exist to show that a later autumn trip was often made from Bideford to fetch manure to fertilise the fields, and then during the winter the ship would be laid up. At Hartland Quay a small museum in one of the port's buildings shows maps, old pictures and documents to demonstrate all this activity, along with the histories of shipwrecks, the geology and wildlife of the area.

Trade from the much more important ports in the Taw and Torridge Estuaries extended much further afield, certainly to all other parts of the British Isles and to the Mediterranean and, during some periods of colonial history, as far away as America. The scene on the quaysides would have been very much more lively than it is today.

Shipbuilding and communications

Many of the small villages along this coast used to have their own shipbuilding yards. The export of clay (via Fremington Quay, tin, slate, fish, agricultural products and even some manufactured products from the hinterland all called for the supply of good strong boats.

Remember that road transport for heavy loads was slow, difficult and expensive until quite recently. Before that, sea transport reigned supreme in terms of efficiency and speed. Good access to sea transport meant easy access to the world's markets, and this is where it all happened. The first shock for the fleet operators of the ports of North Devon and Cornwall, warning of a far-reaching change in the economic life of the South West, was the coming of the railways.

Not very many years ago, Barnstaple was a major junction for railways from Ilfracombe, Bideford, Exeter and Taunton. Barnstaple Junction Station used to stand where the DIY centre is now and, although the current Barnstaple Junction Station does have a two-hourly service from Exeter, this is only a shadow of the days of the great railway era. However, the Barnstaple to Exeter line is being promoted as the scenic 'Tarka Line', a tourist route to the north coast.

The North Devon link road, from the M5 to Barnstaple and on to Bideford, was designed to replace these former economic links to the outside world and to have a major effect on the economy of the area in the future.

Sustainable tourism

Now that much of the older industry has moved away from the area, the ideal opportunity has arisen for quiet holidays in a healthy environment for which there is increasing demand in an ever more stressful world. Industrial archaeology combines with superb and colourful wildlife and landscape and fascinating geology to form a sound basis for sustainable tourism as a substantial employer and money generator for the South West.

Walking, cycling, surfing and other outdoor non-polluting sports, together with efficient public transport, can attract visitors in an environmentally sensitive way. Some accommodation providers are catering for a profitable market in supplying local organic produce, as well as emphasising good care for the environment. Bus services have improved along the route enormously in recent years. Many of our visitors are enquiring about this type of facility before they decide on their holiday location. Traffic-free villages in other countries are attracting an ever-increasing share of this lucrative trade. Projects like the Northern Devon and North Cornwall Coast and Countryside Services, the Exmoor National Park Authority, the Tarka Trail and the South West Coast Path itself have been shown to generate hundreds of millions of pounds for the economy of the South West by attracting visitors who are keen to protect the environment we have all come to enjoy.

Recent research has established that the South West Coast Path alone draws more than a quarter of all the visitors to the coastal strip, who contribute £136m to the local economy, whilst local people in the four counties skirting the route take some 23 million walks along the Coast Path annually, bringing in £116m, and their visiting friends and relatives generate a further £48m.

Leaflets can be obtained about individual aspects of this great effort from the local Tourist Information Centres. Some are listed at the back of this book. Some of the websites can provide information and some will also let you book your accommodation and travel tickets on-line.

7 Westward Ho! to Clovelly

along The Hobby Drive
11 miles (17.9 km)

As you pass the last of the chalets west of Westward Ho! you follow a coastal track which was the old Westward Ho!– Bideford Railway. Keep to this until it branches inland at the end of Cornborough Cliff, where there is a fence across the former railway just after a rock cutting, and then go along the well-trodden cliff top over Abbotsham Cliff, drop down, then rise again over Green Cliff **22**. A seam of anthracite was exploited here in 1805 and used to fire the nearby lime kilns.

The Coast Path continues due south-west, running into a wild hummocky area above dramatic folding formations on the beach below, and then zig-zags up to the summit of the cliff where it strikes south-west again, looking directly towards Buck's Mills, with Clovelly further along.

Westward Ho!, where Rudyard Kipling went to school, viewed from Northam Burrows Pebble Ridge.

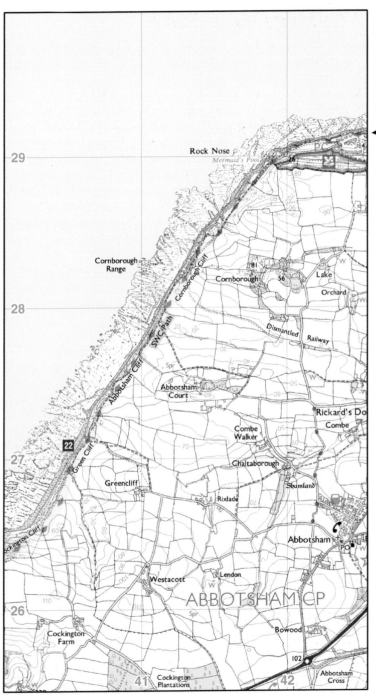

Rock Nose

Mermaid's Pool

Cornborough
Range

Cornborough Cliff

SWC path

Cornborough

Lake

Orchard

Dismantled Railway

Abbotsham Cliff

Abbotsham
Court

Rickard's Do

Combe

Spr

Combe
Walker

Chaltaborough

Sbamland

Green Cliff

Greencliff

Rixlade

Cockington Cliff

Westacott

Lendon

Abbotsham

PO

ABBOTSHAM CP

Spr

Bowood

Cockington
Farm

Cockington
Plantations

Abbotsham
Cross

Contours are given in metres
The vertical interval is 10m

The path now crosses a substantial Devon field boundary to continue south-west along the cliff top, then begins to drop steeply into the combe just north of Westacott Cliff, descending a series of steps at the mouth of the stream **A**. Here it crosses the pebble beach for 15–20 yards before zig-zagging back towards the top of the cliff via a wooden staircase.

Follow the top of Westacott Cliff and dip down to another stream before passing through a delightful thicket of willow, hawthorn and hazel, where the speckled wood butterfly is in residence. A carpet of woodland flowers clothes the ground. You emerge from this on to Higher Rowden, where the path follows the clifftop slopes just outside the field fence. Cross one stream by the footbridge, continuing along the cliff top all the way to Peppercombe. At Peppercombe the path comes through a bridle-gate onto a stone track. (This is a lovely spot to stop for a rest by the stream, or if you go up the track it's a 15 minute walk to Horns Cross, The Coach and Horses pub and a post office/village store.) The Coast Path crosses the combe on an old stone bridge and then turns left up into the woods, whilst a second gate leads down to the beach. The Coast Path then branches briefly inland across the combe to climb back towards the sea, crossing the remains of the earthwork at Peppercombe Castle at the top.

Carry on through Sloo Wood and enter Worthygate Wood. The path zig-zags very steeply down to Buck's Mills, arriving at the village street above the beach. A visit to the rocky beach is worthwhile. The steep incline was built to take loads of lime brought across from the Welsh coast opposite and processed in the lime kilns, one of which is buttressed and so substantial

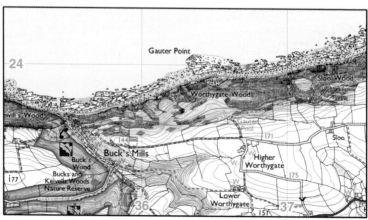

Contours are given in metres
The vertical interval is 5m

that it could be mistaken for a ruined castle. The boats were, and still are, landed and launched straight from the beach.

To continue, take a small pathway west, which has stone steps a few yards from the road from your arrival point. This rises into Buck's Wood, part of the nature reserve, where a narrow track zig-zags up the side of the valley and then turns right towards the cliffs to emerge into a more open area with newly planted trees.

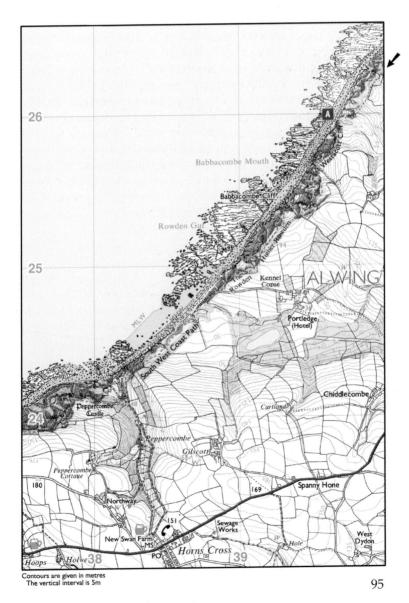

Contours are given in metres
The vertical interval is 5m

95

Continue along the clifftop path in some more woodland, keeping due west below Walland Cary, an old stately home that is now a holiday centre. Walland Cary inherited its name from Henry de la Wallen, lord of the manor in the reign of Edward I in the late 13th century.

The path is well marked as it winds up and down through this wild and ancient wood, keeping parallel to the sea. Then it rises and goes inland to emerge into the clifftop fields. Turn right and keep going along the seaward edge of the field until the path leads back into the woods. The path keeps inside the wood, curving left and back to the clifftop slopes, then emerges into fields again. At the far western side of the second field, turn inland for another hundred yards or so and then go back into the woods and down to a bridge over a small stream. The path climbs steeply out of the ravine and you turn right on to The Hobby Drive. Turn westwards and follow this drive through the woods for the next 2 miles (3 km).

The Hobby Drive was built in the early 19th century under the direction of the owner, Sir James Hamlyn Williams. Such projects were often started to occupy Napoleonic prisoners of war, or to provide employment during times of economic depression.

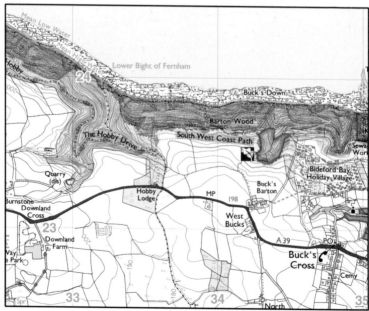

2 km or 1 mile   Contours are given in metres
Woolfardisworthy   The vertical interval is 5m

Clovelly, where the young Charles Kingsley's father was rector, seen from The Hobby Drive.

In spite of its reputation as a tourist trap, there is no escaping the fact that Clovelly is unique. Therefore, although the Coast Path continues well above the village, I heartily recommend a shortcut signed down to the village just before the western end of The Hobby Drive, visiting the harbour and then ascending the steep cobbled village street. There are pubs, tea houses and a number of places that offer bed and breakfast.

One family, the Careys of Clovelly, owned this area for 400 years, from the 14th to the 18th century, building and maintaining the famous stone pier that made a safe haven for the local fishing boats to set out to sea for shoals of herring. In 1730 the estate was sold to Zachary Hamlyn whose descendants have managed it since.

The church at Clovelly is also worth a visit. It has a Jacobean pulpit and a memorial to Charles Kingsley. The Reverend Charles Kingsley Senior came here as parish priest when his son was about 11. Apparently, the older Kingsley was a good sailor and skilful fisherman, and when the fishing fleet went to sea he would descend to the quay to conduct a parting service.

Marine wildlife found on the North Devon and Cornwall coasts

Coastal walking offers a unique opportunity to explore both terrestrial and marine wildlife. It is well worth taking the time to look seawards and consider the wealth of life beneath the waves. Walking with an aqualung in your rucksack might be a little impractical, but the large tidal range that is a feature of this coast gives plenty of scope for exploring the seashores on foot. Where the path plunges down to sea level, take a breather and see what you can find in the rock pools.

The marine inhabitants of this stretch of coast certainly do not have an easy life. They must withstand the full force of an Atlantic swell and the drying effects of the wind and the sun. The small white barnacles that encrust the rocks thrive on wave action. They are close relatives of shrimps and prawns and, although they are cemented to the rocks, they filter food from passing water with their legs. The blue-black mussels, however, prefer a more sheltered home and can often be found in crevices on the landward side of the rocks and boulders. Round, flat limpet shells are a familiar sight and an ideal shape for hanging on to the rock. They graze algae from the rock surface and always return 'home', where they fit the rock perfectly.

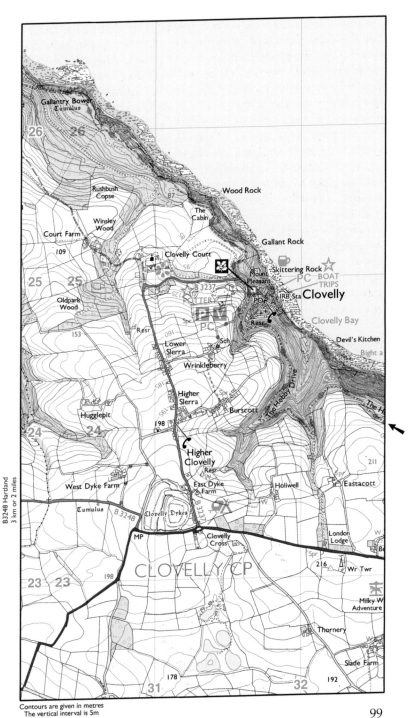

Gallantry Bower
Tumulus

26   26

Rushbush
Copse

Wood Rock

Winsley
Wood

The
Cabin

Court Farm

Gallant Rock

109

Clovelly Court

Skittering Rock
PC   BOAT
TRIPS

25   25

Oldpark
Wood

Mount
Pleasant
B 3237
SCH
POTTERY

PO
IRB Sta   Clovelly

153

Resr

PH
PC

Resr

Clovelly Bay

091

Sch

Devil's Kitchen

Lower
Sierra

Bight a

Wrinkleberry

185

Higher
Sierra

Spr

Hugglepit

561

Burscott

The Hobby Drive

24   24

198

The H

Higher
Clovelly

Resr

211

West Dyke Farm

East Dyke
Farm

Holiwell

Eastacott

Tumulus

B 3248

Clovelly Dykes

B 3237

Clovelly
Cross

London
Lodge

B

MP

23   23

CLOVELLY CP

216   Wr Twr

198

Milky W
Adventure

Thornery

31   178

32   192

Slade Farm

B3248 Hartland
3 km or 2 miles

Contours are given in metres
The vertical interval is 5m

99

These, and other shellfish, often fall prey to the dog whelk, which drills a hole through the shell and sucks out the unfortunate victim! Dog whelk eggs, like rows of small yellow milk bottles on the undersides of the rocks, are also a common sight. The beadlet anemone, like a blob of jelly, withdraws its stinging tentacles while the tide is out. All three colour forms of this anemone – green, red and 'strawberry' – occur along this coast.

Seaweeds, high up on the shore, tend to be stunted by the pounding waves. In rock pools, however, they make a colourful garden. The pink, encrusting weed and the coarse, tufted coralline weed contrast with the bright green and brown weeds. If you are fortunate enough to visit one of the many rocky shores at a very low tide, you will glimpse the kelp forest below low-water mark. Among these huge, strap-like seaweeds, urchins, starfish, sea-slugs, sponges, crabs and lobsters make their homes. Pollock, wrasse, conger and bass shelter among the kelp. These provide food for seabirds, such as puffins, gannets and cormorants, and for the grey seals that breed in the caves and bays of Hartland and Lundy.

This coast is fed by the Gulf Stream and therefore can boast several marine creatures that are not found on other parts of the English coast. The snakelocks anemone, with its long, wavy tentacles, is a common sight in rock pools but the dahlia anemone, with its striped tentacles and sticky column, covered with shell fragments, is a rare find.

Rocks and rock pools often occur alongside sandy shores, which appear barren in comparison. The sand is constantly scoured by the waves, so its inhabitants live safely buried beneath the surface. Shells cast up on the shore give an idea of what lives below. A walk after a storm can reveal some fascinating finds: egg cases of skate or dogfish (mermaid's purses), cuttlefish bones and goose barnacles covering plastic containers.

The estuaries at either end of this path support a wealth of fascinating wildlife, influenced by fresh and salt water. The mudflats, exposed at low tide, and the saltmarsh areas support many plants, shellfish and worms, which in turn provide food for birds. The Taw and Torridge Estuaries are of national and regional importance for wintering wildfowl and waders: wigeon, shelduck, oystercatcher, golden and ringed plover, redshank and curlew, to mention just a few. In the sheltered uppershore regions of the estuaries, periwinkles and seaweeds such as bladderwrack and eggwrack, more familiar on rocky beaches, cling to pebbles and empty shells surprisingly far upriver. The balance of life is delicate in this estuarine community and is therefore highly vulnerable to pollution.

Another interesting feature of the estuaries are the sand dunes, found on the seaward margins. Coarse marram grass binds the sand together on the newer dunes. The intermediate ridges are colonised by other plants until they become grass-covered and grazed by rabbits. In the damp slacks between the ridges grow scrub plants, such as blackthorn, and this is an excellent place for wild flowers and insects. The Braunton Burrows area is an international Biosphere Reserve. Some plants such as the tiny French toadflax grow nowhere else in Britain.

Created in 1994, the North Devon Voluntary Marine Conservation Area is one of the two VMCAs run by the Devon Wildlife Trust. It stretches for about 21 miles (34 km) from Hangman Point in the east to Down End in Croyde in the west, extending from the cliff base seawards to the 20-metre depth contour. It is home to the rare and beautiful scarlet and gold star coral and the shy leopard spotted goby – a small fish. In summer, the strange-looking sunfish and the giant basking shark can often be seen off this stretch of coast.

It is an exciting time for coastal management. The lessons learned through pioneering work on the Heritage Coasts are now being applied on a wider scale. Management is being achieved by co-operation between coastal interests through voluntary groups, and coastal managers are being encouraged to 'look out to the sea' and consider the *whole* coast as an ecologically integrated entity.

8 Clovelly to Hartland Quay

passing Gallantry Bower and Windbury Waterfall
10¹/₄ miles (16.5 km)

Going westwards from Clovelly is not quite as straightforward as it looks on many maps. If you are emerging from The Hobby Drive where the steep, small cobbled track from the village meets the road, go north along the road for a short distance. One road then turns inland and another leads seawards **A**. Go through the wooden gate into the field between the roads at this fork and skirt round the lower, seaward, side of the field. Go to the right of a small knowle, where the path is overlooking the wooded clifftop slopes above the sea. At the far end go through the metal kissing-gate into the next field. Keep close to the woods until you come to another gate that takes you into woodland, emerging at 'The Cabin'.

For the next half mile (800 metres), the path keeps parallel to the steeply sloping top of the cliff. The route runs through

Clovelly's pier, built to the orders of one George Carey, lawyer, in the 16th century, used to shelter a fleet of 60 fishing boats.

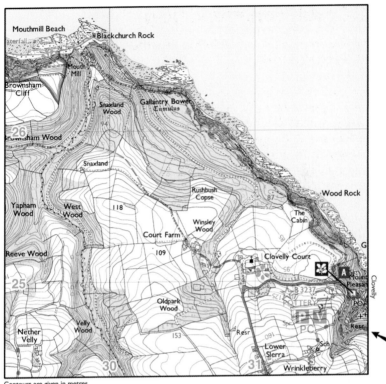

Contours are given in metres
The vertical interval is 5m

woodland and takes you past several more intriguing shelters, one, dated 1826, with carved wooden angel's wings.

Currently a nature conservation scheme is taking place at Gallantry Bower to reduce overgrowth and restore certain types of wildlife to the cliff top, so the appearance may be more open than I have described here.

From Gallantry Bower (325 feet/100 metres) in height), the path first clings to the cliff top, and then goes sharp right down a very steep, overgrown slope. As it enters more mature woodland it zig-zags down to the forest track which leads to Mouthmill Beach and its lime kiln. On the rocky beach is Blackchurch Rock, with its two natural archways.

Continuing westwards, cross the stream by the stepping stones and go up the grass track inland, past the lime kiln and a building that was once a tea house. Find a path climbing right up through the woods, emerging at the top of a very steep slope into a field with superb views of Blackchurch Rock and the North Devon coast.

103

Keep to the seaward side of the fields, parallel to the sea, until you come to a stile on National Trust property leading to the steep zig-zag path down to Windbury Waterfall **B**. At the bottom of this valley, and very close to the sea and cliff top, cross the wooden footbridge. On the western side of this a track leads upstream and inland for about a hundred yards before the Coast Path returns northwards to the cliff top. There it turns westwards to reach Windbury Head and its prehistoric earthwork at 468 feet (135 metres). The prominent red outcrop is Exmansworthy Cliff. The National Trust has signed paths connecting the Coast Path with their car park at Exmansworthy Farm just inland.

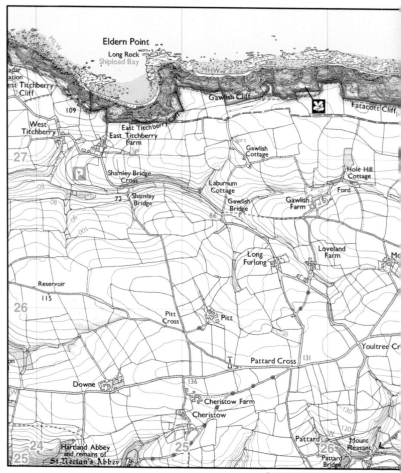

Contours are given in metres
The vertical interval is 5m

2 km or 1 m
Hartland

There are no major climbs or descents from here until you reach Hartland Point, approximately 4 miles (6.4 km) away. However, between Hartland Point and Hartland Quay there is some more climbing and descent to be done.

Keep just inside the fields on Fatacott Cliff until you come to a National Trust sign for Gawlish, from where the Coast Path winds past some small terraced fields. Just east of Shipload Bay the path stays outside the fence, clinging to the top of East Titchberry Cliff. Here it meets a bridleway running east–west, which you follow west. The bridleway bends sharply south to East Titchberry, and here the Coast Path goes seawards before entering the fields and keeping to the cliff top.

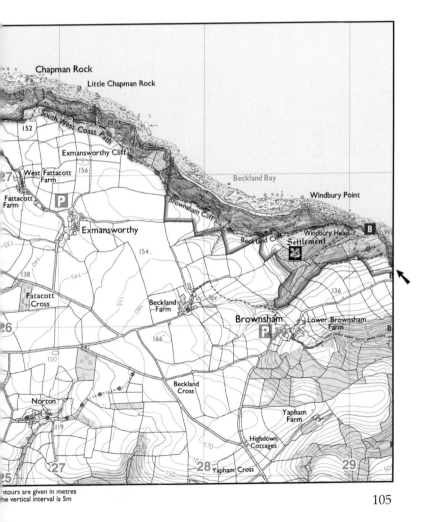

Just to the east of Hartland Point **23** the Coast Path is outside the fence. After passing to the seaward side of the mushroom-shaped radar tower you will see a small car park with a tea kiosk, open at Easter and then from May to September.

To continue west, leave the car park by the Lighthouse Road past a notice saying 'No Unauthorised Vehicles'. Note the water collection system: a large area of concrete that feeds into a tank on the opposite side of the road. It used to supply water to the lighthouse. Also note the Trinity House property waymark boundary. Just past a small, square, flat-roofed storeroom, the Coast Path turns west up a steep concrete path with some steps and a wicket-gate, and then makes for the tall square of security barbed-wire fencing surrounding a coastguard lookout, now manned only on an occasional basis. The Coast Path continues south-west, down from the headland, and follows the cliffs.

Rock strata etched out by the Atlantic waves below Upright Cliff. The complex geology here is best studied from the Coast Path.

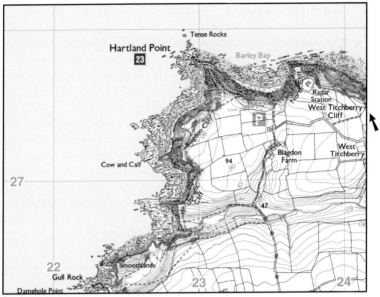

Contours are given in metres
The vertical interval is 5m

Suddenly, a view southwards opens up, with Damehole Point and Gull Rock standing out prominently across two small coves, and a strange, lonely, wild little valley behind, called Smoothlands. The Coast Path runs along Upright Cliff and then descends steeply to Titchberry Water, where there is a path down to the beach.

Make your way upstream to the footbridge across Titchberry Water, with a stile on each side, then climb a flight of wooden steps. At the top of the steep slope the Coast Path goes seawards, parallel with the stream below, with a high hedgewall on the southern side. Going south and west now the path leaves the edge of the field and descends into Smoothlands. It keeps along the bottom of this old hanging valley, which evidently was once the bed of the stream that now runs into the cover to the north. The valley floor is covered in gorse and bracken with small outcrops of heather and stonecrop and some giant ant hills.

Soon you come to a number of stepping stones over a marshy spot, beyond which is a small rocky cove. This is Damehole Point, halfway between Hartland Point and Hartland Quay. Go up the slope on the southern side of Smoothlands Valley and you will see Stoke Church tower **24** and also a tower that stands behind Hartland Quay. Beware of the holes near the edge of the cliff where there is serious subsidence. This is Blegberry Cliff and the Coast Path stays close to it, dropping steeply down into Blegberry Water, with its waterfall, before rising steeply to the top of a sheer slab of rock 650 feet (200 metres) above the sea.

Stoke Church **24** (worth visiting from Hartland Quay if you have time) can be seen once again at the head of the valley of Hartland Abbey (Abbey and Gardens open to the public). Descend into the valley, go behind the cottage just back from the beach, and cross a small bridge to the east of it. The cottage was Blackpool Mill and the river is called the Abbey River. Go through an iron kissing-gate just behind the cottages, and upstream for about a hundred yards to cross the bridge. Then turn back immediately towards the coast and climb due south just inland of Dyer's Lookout.

Continuing south and west you soon come to the top of Warren Cliff and within site of Hartland Quay **25**.

Keep back from the cliff top, go just in front of the rocket apparatus house, and take a track and then the small road leading down to the quay. Here there is a pub with accommodation, and well-illustrated displays in the attic room above the shop of Hartland Quay's fascinating trading history, geology and marine wildlife. A visit to the Hartland Quay Museum, open more or less between spring and autumn half-terms inclusive, and by request to B&B residents, is recommended.

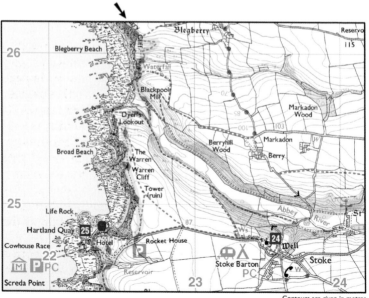

Contours are given in metres
The vertical interval is 5m

Hartland Quay from Damehole Point. Visit the museum at Hartland Quay for a fascinating picture of this area's past.

The history of Hartland Quay

There was a harbour at Hartland Quay until the end of the 19th century, when the railway reached Bideford and road transport improved, so it became uneconomic to repair storm damage and keep up the quay. If you have walked this section of coast during stormy weather you will be amazed that any man-made structure managed to survive the 300 years that it did. It is supposed that the massive rocks used for its foundations were roped to sealed empty barrels, moved into position at high tide and the ropes cut in the appropriate place to bed the stone in.

During the 17th century the property passed to the Luttrells of Dunster and it is assumed that at this time the Merchants House and stores, which still stand, and the lime kiln at the quay, were built.

In the middle of the 19th century Hartland Quay supported several families of workers, servants, a coastguard, a publican and possibly a maltster.

9 Hartland Quay to Bude

via Higher Sharpnose Point
15 1/4 miles (24.5 km)

To continue south, retrace your steps from the quay and enter the clifftop car park on the right. Go to the far corner and then across a small valley to continue along the cliff top. A few hundred yards to the south of Hartland Quay you will see the promontory of Screda Point with its sheer, jagged plates of slate thrusting out of the sea.

The Coast Path skirts round the landward side of St Catherine's Tor and crosses a stream on some round concrete stepping stones. The former dam behind the high stone boundary was the swan pool for Hartland Abbey. Make for a wicket-gate in the wall opposite. Having gone through the wicket-gate, turn seawards along the wall for about 20 yards and then strike south at a 45-degree angle up the slope, to emerge on the cliff top where it overlooks yet another rocky bay. Rise again to 200 feet (60 metres) round the back of this bay and cross the field boundary stile.

The stony path becomes narrower and steeper, and drops on a zig-zag down to the flat area around the waterfalls at Speke's Mill Mouth. In summer the meadow through which you pass is covered in eyebright, yarrow and wood sage, with little clumps of heather and milkwort. Go along the track upstream for 200 yards (180 metres) and cross the footbridge. Now go south-west up a valley that runs up the landward side of Swansford Hill. When you get to the top of the valley the path once more follows the cliff top.

After the next mile (1.6 km) the Coast Path comes to a ditch. For the youth hostel **26**, strike inland and slightly back on the northern side of this ditch, through a gateway with a stile, then keep along the farm track straight ahead until you come to the phone box at Elmscott. Turn right (south) and you reach the youth hostel.

If you are continuing, keep south along the clifftop path and go to the landward side of a sunken triangular field. Keep on the level and make for the stile at the far edge of the higher land above, which brings you out on a country lane. Turn right (south-west) and continue down this lane for 600 yards (500 metres) before turning right (west) over a stile and seawards along a field boundary, where you come to the cliff top again.

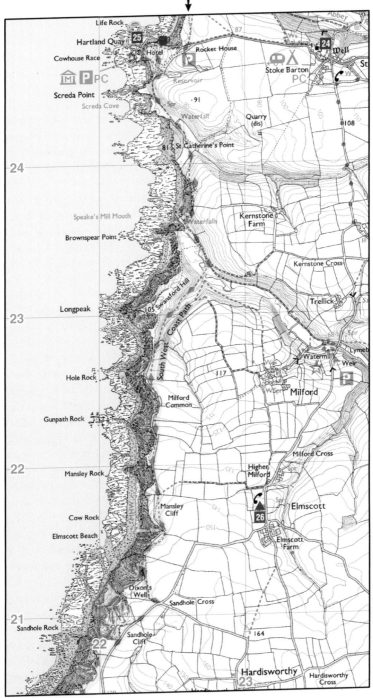

Contours are given in metres
The vertical interval is 5m

Basically, the Coast Path now follows the cliff top the whole way to Bude, rising frequently to about 500 feet (150 metres), then dipping to sea level, only to rise again on the other side of the valley. You should be a good deal fitter when you get to the other end! Going south you will see the buildings of South Hole Farm 300 yards (275 metres) inland.

Go over the stile by the National Trust sign for South Hole and the path rises gently to the Iron Age ramparts at the hill fort of Embury Beacon **27** (515 feet/157 metres). The promontory forts at Hillsborough, east of Ilfracombe, the most distinct example on this path, and the defensive earthworks above Sillery, between Countisbury and Lynton, would be of a similar age. Elsewhere along the path there is evidence of two other main periods of pre-medieval occupation. The many small mounds can be assumed to be evidence of a Bronze Age civilisation, and the standing stones near the Coast Path, particularly between Lee and Mortehoe, were probably erected during the same period. You may also remember the Roman fortlet at Martinhoe (page 48), with the remains of barrack buildings, field ovens at the back of the earth ramparts, an armourers' furnace and evidence of the signal fires on the cliff top. At Tintagel Church there are Roman boundary markers, referred to locally as milestones.

Half a mile (1 km) south of Embury, the path passes Knap Head and comes to a stile where you leave the NT South Hole property, keep along the fence, and turn right down the steep slope directly towards Welcombe Mouth, where there is a small car park and some sand on the beach. Cross the stream just above the waterfalls by the round stepping stones and leave on a narrow path from the southern end of the car park. You now climb to 330 feet (100 metres). Cross the field on its landward side across stiles and you are soon overlooking Marsland Mouth, a reserve managed jointly by the Devon and Cornwall Wildlife Trusts. The path emerges from the southern side of the valley in a wide zigzag sweep. Just below is the poet Ronald Duncan's hut, with a welcome sign on the door inviting you in when it is unlocked. Find out all about him inside. As you cross the footbridge over the stream you enter Cornwall. Note the mill wheel on West Mill **28** just upstream. Rise again to 400 feet (122 metres) at Marsland Cliff where the path runs very close to the cliff top.

The next steep valley to negotiate is Litter Mouth, where the Coast Path descends on wooden steps and zig-zags back up to the cliff top. Follow the cliff top to Yeolmouth Cliff (500ft/150m) and look back north at Gull Rock **29**, which has a square hole

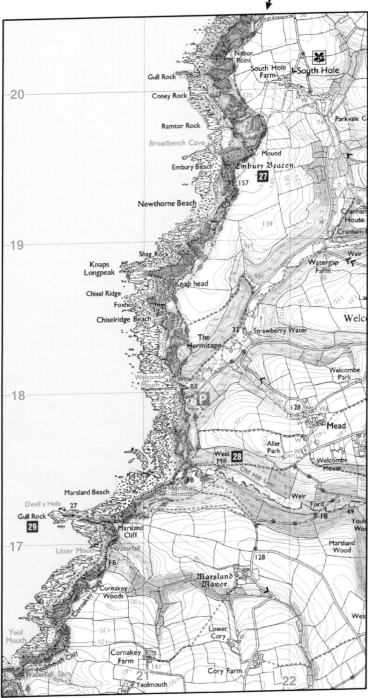

South Hole
Nabor Point
South Hole Farm
Gull Rock
Coney Rock
Parkvale C
Ramtor Rock
Broadbench Cove
Mound
Embury Beach
Embury Beacon
157
27
139
Cranham House
Cranham F
Newthorne Beach
Shag Rock
Spr
Weir
Knaps Longpeak
Watergap Farm
La
Knap head
Chisel Ridge
Foxhold
Welc
Chiselridge Beach
33
Strawberry Water
The Hermitage
Welcombe Park
Welcombe Mouth
Waterfall
BS
P
28
Mead
Aller Park
West Mill
28
Welcombe House
Old Mill Leat
FB
Marsland Mouth
Marsland Beach
Weir
Ford
Devil's Hole
27
FB
49
Gull Rock
29
Marsland Cliff
Youl
Woo
Litter Mouth
Marsland Wood
Waterfall
FB
128
Cornakey C
Cornakey Woods
Marsland Manor
Yeol Mouth
Lower Cory
Wes
Yeolmouth Cliff
Cornakey Farm
141
Waterfall Spr.
21
Cory Farm
22
Yeolmouth

Contours are given in metres
The vertical interval is 5m

113

through it called Devil's Hole. Then there is another dip into Yeolmouth and a rise to Henna Cliff. If you come down from Henna Cliff into Morwenstow, look carefully at the vicarage building to the left of the church **30**. The eccentric Parson Hawker, who came here as vicar in 1834, replaced the derelict vicarage with a mock Gothic structure, adding his own mark with strange chimneys representing the towers of various churches. He is credited with starting the Harvest Festival service and wrote the Cornish anthem 'Shall Trelawney Die'.

As you scramble down into the deep valley, you will see a fine selection of plants characteristic of the area: heather, scabious, sea carrot, kidney vetch, birdsfoot trefoil, sea campion and stonecrop. Here, while the Coast Path is still within sight of the tower of Morwenstow, a path from the village joins it.

Just to the south of this you will come to a National Trust sign saying 'Hawker's Hut' **31**. Go down a few steps and you will see a wooden-doored, wooden-walled, wooden-seated, turf-covered hut nestling under sea-thrift and stonecrop and giving a magnificent view out to sea. Hawker was the vicar of Morwenstow for 40 years. He used driftwood to build his hut and, wearing a fisherman's jumper of the special Morwenstow knit pattern and boots, in addition to his cassock, he used it as a place of meditation, wrote some of his poetry here, and occasionally enjoyed an opium pipe.

As you approach Higher Sharpnose Point you will see a stream called The Tidna. The path zig-zags down to Tidna Shute (NT), crosses a bridge, then a stile and turns seawards to rise diagonally towards the summit of Higher Sharpnose Point. You go past a disused coastguard station and turn up southeast along a tiny valley which runs parallel to the cliff edge.

After ¾ of a mile (1 km) you come to Stanbury Mouth, where you have to zig-zag briefly inland and back to the footbridge, mount wooden steps and continue south straight up the hill. From Stanbury Mouth there is also a path inland. The Coast Path takes you near the Composite Signals Organisation Station at Cleave Camp, where massive satellite-tracking dish aerials dominate the coastal scene. As you get halfway along the seaward side of the boundary fence of this establishment, turn sharply seawards across the grass without dropping too much, to enjoy the views from Lower Sharpnose Point, and then keep on south along the gorse-covered cliff top.

When you reach the very steep slope overlooking the Coombe Valley, look inland to see Kilkhampton Church standing

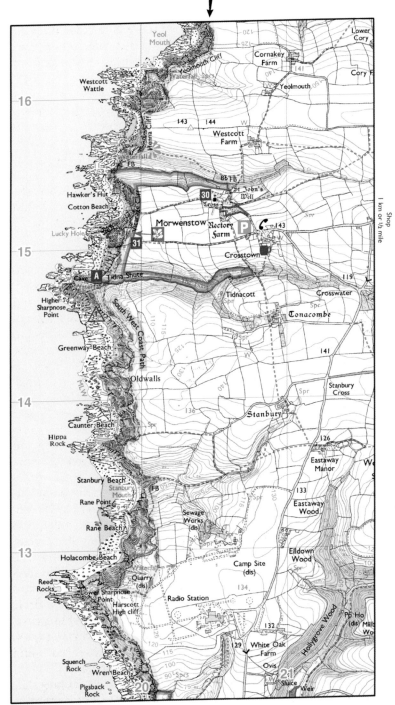

Contours are given in metres
The vertical interval is 5m

Coombe Valley. The farm at Stowe Barton (centre top) was the site of a great mansion built in the Restoration period .

on the hill at the end of the valley. From the 12th to the 18th centuries nearly all the fields you can see from Steeple Point belonged to the Grenville family. This family became famous during the Tudor and Stuart reigns, and Roger Grenville was captain of the *Mary Rose*. The galleon sank off Portsmouth in 1545, with King Henry VIII looking on, and has now been raised and put on display in Portsmouth. Other members of the family played prominent roles in the Army and Navy during the 16th and 17th centuries. One of the last of the family to achieve fame was John Grenville, who helped greatly in the Restoration of the Stuart monarchy. As a result he became Earl of Bath, Governor of Plymouth, and Lord Lieutenant of Cornwall and was able to build a large four-storey mansion. If you look across the valley you will see a group of farm buildings. This was the site of his house **32**, demolished only 60 years after it had been built because Sir John's sister preferred to live elsewhere.

If you look upstream towards the top of the meadow you will see a small stone road bridge **33**. Parson Hawker took note of the locals' concern that the stream here was often difficult to ford. He started a subscription list and made a request to the King, who began the fund with a donation of £20. It is called King William's Bridge and was completed in 1836. From your clifftop viewpoint overlooking the Coombe Valley you can take the public footpath down to the road or follow the Coast Path out to the tip of Steeple Point and back down to the beach on an existing cliff-edge path with a superb overview of the coast to the south.

Going south from Duckpool the path climbs in a wide zigzag sweep to the top of Warren Point before dropping to Warren Gutter, where a stream drops down to a rocky beach where the rock formations are exposed horizontally. Continuing along the cliff top for another half mile (1 km) south, the Coast Path comes to Sandy Mouth where there is a National Trust car park, refreshments in season, and toilets.

All the way from Duckpool to Bude there are sandy beaches at low tide. Bathing can be dangerous, however, particularly at low tide when the coastal currents can be very strong. Please observe any warning notices, flags or lifeguard instructions. It is generally safer to swim on an incoming tide than an outgoing one.

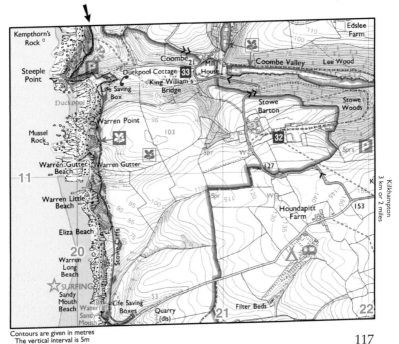

Contours are given in metres
The vertical interval is 5m

South of Sandy Mouth, past Menachurch Point (note the Bronze Age tumulus **34**), the Coast Path follows the cliff top to Crooklets Beach and from there stays close to the sea along a permissive path until you come alongside the River Neet in Bude. Cross the first bridge you come to and carry straight on down the street opposite. Turn right (north-west) when you come to the second stretch of water which is the old Bude Canal. After visiting Bude Stratton Museum on the quay, walk seawards until you reach the canal lock. Cross the lock and continue to follow the cliff top towards Efford Down.

The tramway on the Canal Basin at Bude. The canal was built in 1823 to take calcium-rich beach sand from Bude to inland farms.

BUDE BAY

Long Rock

Bethams

Sarshall's Pit
Dunsmouth Farm

Westpark Pit

34 Tumulus
Menachurch Point
Bucket Hill
Linhaye

Curtis's Rock

Northcott Mouth

☆ SURFING

Smooth Rock

Tumulus

Maer Down

Wrangle Point

Crooklets

Crooklets Beach

PC

☆ SURFING

Coach Rock

IRB Sta (summer only)
Bude Haven
FB   Lock

Compass Point

Tower

Hotel

Ebbingford Manor

Efford Beacon

Efford Down

Higher Northcott
Lower Northcott
Little Northcott

Tor View
Grenville Gate

The Bungalow
Bude Holiday Park

Maer

Rosemerrin

Nature Reserve

Tumulus

Hotel   Sch

Summerleaze Down   Flexbury

CYCLE HIRE
CH

Swimming Pool

Weir

Liby   FB
Pol Sta

Hotel

V i

Pen Dene   Moor

Moor Cross Cottages

Trelana

Reeds

Mayfield

Paize

Broomhill Manor

Broomhill Lane

Burn Park

BUDE-STRATTON CP

School

Superstore

BUDE

School

A3072   Coast

Cleavelands

Moat   Binhamy

Pou
52

River Neet

contours are given in metres
the vertical interval is 5m

119

10 Bude to Boscastle Harbour

via Pencannow and Crackington Haven
16¹/₂ miles (26.5 km)

It would be difficult to get lost on the next stretch of the Coast Path to Widemouth. It hugs the cliff top and the back of the beaches all the way and runs alongside the Bude–Widemouth road for part of its length. Simply follow the low cliff top until you are just half a mile (1 km) south of Widemouth.

A CIRCULAR WALK FROM BUDE

6 miles (9.7 km)
(see map opposite)

Park in the town and cross the River Neet. Make your way alongside the canal which runs west of the river towards the sea. Note lines which are still in place from the tramway, used to transfer goods from moored sea-going boats to the canal barges. The Castle between the canal and the river was built by Sir Goldsworthy Gurney, the Cornish engineer responsible for one of the earliest steam locomotives.

Cross the lock and turn right and follow the road seawards until you see a wicket-gate. Go through this on to the open cliff top and make for Compass Point, so-called because of the folly there adorned with the points of the compass. Looking up the coast to the north you may see the one-acre saltwater swimming pool, built in the late 1800s after the railway started bringing ever larger numbers of visitors, and still well used.

Keep on along the cliffs until you come to Lower Longbeak, overlooking Widemouth Sand. There is a car park here to give access to the headland. Just north of the salt house, which is the first house to come between the cliffs and the Coast Path after leaving Bude, make for the road and a stile and gate giving access to a path across the fields. Go north-east to the top corner of the field and straight ahead for the far side of the next field. Follow the next field boundary, and then head north-east again to join a drive leading to a bridge over a stream. Just before the bridge turn left along a permissive path and join the canal towpath. Follow this back into Bude.

You could also start this walk from Lower Longbeak car park just north of Widemouth. There are information points along the path which explain the history of the canal.

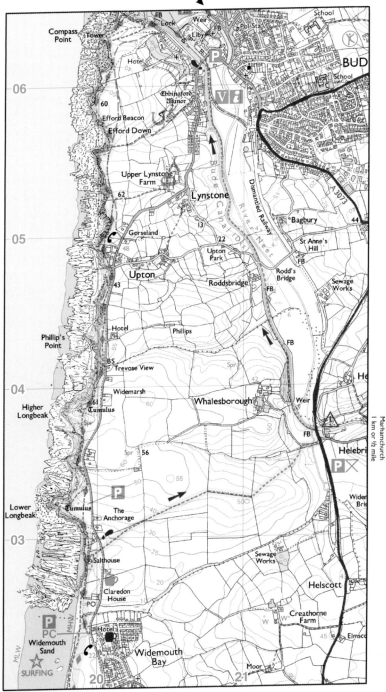

Contours are given in metres
The vertical interval is 5m

121

You are now approaching Wanson Mouth where the cliffs have crumbled, necessitating a detour inland **A** along a track that joins the coast road. Follow the coast road, which has been reconstructed to avoid the landslips, for ³/₄ mile (1.3 km) southwest. At this point **B** the road turns inland and the Coast Path stays on the cliff top at Bridwill Point, turning south and away from the cliffs only on the steep descent into Millook. Join the road again at Millook to go west up the steep bit, glancing back to note the extraordinary chevron folding of the cliffs here. Keep to the cliffs where the road turns inland 300 yards (275 metres) up the hill at Raven's Beak. The Coast Path now stays on the cliff top, passing above Dizzard Wood with its dwarf oaks and nationally important lichens, all the way to Crackington Haven, with one 250-foot (75 metre) fall and rise just south of Chipman Point.

Between Castle Point, just north of Crackington Haven, and Trebarwith Strand there are several places where it is extremely dangerous to stray from the path. Large, slippery slabs of shale or steep screes end either in rough seas or at precipice tops, and there is sometimes no way out of these areas once entered. For safe

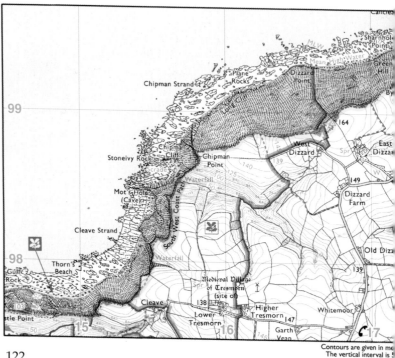

Contours are given in me
The vertical interval is !

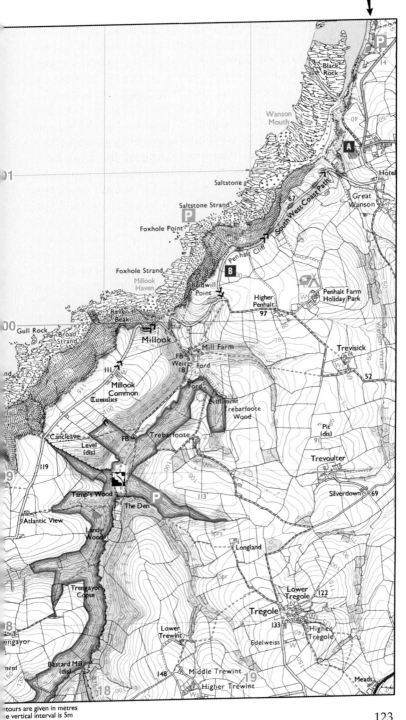

Black Rock

Wanson Mouth

A

Hotel

Saltstone

South West Coast Path

Great Wanson

Saltstone Strand

P

Foxhole Point

Penhalt Cliff

B

Foxhole Strand

Millook Haven

Buildwill Point

Higher Penhalt
97

Penhalt Farm Holiday Park

Raven's Beak

Gull Rock

Broad Strand

Millook

Mill Farm

Trevisick

52

FB
Weir
18   Ford

Millook Common
Tumulus

Ford

Settlement

Trebarfoote Wood

Pit
(dis)
91

Cancleave

Level
(dis)

FB

Trebarfoote

Trevoulter

119

Silverdown   69

Tamp's Wood

The Den

P

113

Atlantic View

Landy Wood

Sprs

Longland

Spr

Trengayor Copse

Lower Tregole   122

Tregole

133

Lower Trewint

Higher Tregole

engayor

Edelweiss

Bastard Mill
(dis)

148   Middle Trewint
19
Higher Trewint

Meads

18

tours are given in metres
e vertical interval is 5m

123

walking, caution is therefore advised. Always follow signs and, if in doubt, take the highest route, keeping away from the cliff edge.

At Castle Point keep to the clifftop ridge **C** and then zig-zag down to the stream at Aller Shoot. Then up the zig-zag path on the headland at Pencannow and descend to Crackington Haven.

From Crackington Haven, follow the clifftop path to the south of the beach for half a mile (1 km), when you will be close to Cambeak. Here **D** make absolutely sure that you stay on the cliff top. There is a path marked going lower, but this has fallen away and is dangerous. Turn south to continue over Cambeak. There is also a permissive path through the small valley behind Cambeak. Continue along the cliff top for a further half a mile (1 km).

Just south of The Strangles, near Trevigue Farm, the Coast Path crosses a hummocky area and then drops into a small valley before rising along the side of the clifftop meadows to High Cliff at over 700 feet (223 metres). To the south of High Cliff, the path descends steeply down steps through the gorse until it meets a small stream which runs on the far side of a wall. Go seawards for about 20 yards, where you will find a footbridge that provides an easy crossing point **E**.

The next section can be dangerous if you get too low and near any screes or slate slabs. If you do, you have taken a wrong turning. Whenever in doubt, keep up and away from the cliff edge. Go seawards from the footbridge **E** for 30 yards and then follow a small ridge away from the sea and uphill. Then follow the very narrow path, keeping more or less level around the steep slope above the sea. This path soon curves round to head south, and begins to rise along the bracken-, gorse- and heather-covered slopes, dipping briefly before coming up through a small gap between bracken-covered rocks. The path then turns left and upwards facing into a col, and then right to continue south-west in a steady climb to the crest of the heather-covered slopes. *Ignore any small tracks which go off seawards* and climb steadily to the top.

From the top of Rusey Cliff, the path keeps level round the back of the next hanging valley and along the edge of the fields to Buckator.

After passing Buckator, you will look back to see this sheer black cliff with white bands of quartz running through it, standing next to Gull Rock, one of many on this coast with the same name, with the seething gulley between. West and ahead, you will notice a series of fingers of land and, just offshore, white foam surrounding a number of rocks submerged at high

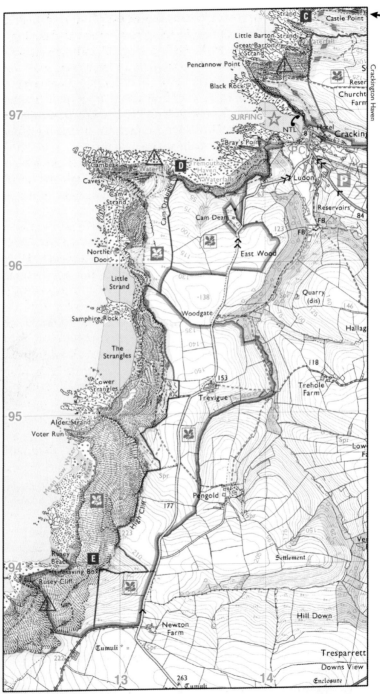

Contours are given in metres
The vertical interval is 5m

tide. These are called Saddle Rock and Beeny Sisters and if you are lucky you may see seals here.

After Buckator descend to cross a wooden footbridge and stepping stones over a marshy hanging valley. Along here the path sticks mainly to the edge of the clifftop fields and more or less on the level, occasionally venturing just outside and crossing substantial stiles to do so. Quite suddenly you will see ahead and to the south a magnificent panorama stretching from Boscastle to Tintagel, with Pentire Head and Trevose Head in the distance. The path drops abruptly down to the low Beeny Cliff.

Steps have been cut in the slate at the top and wooden steps take you on down the steepest bits westwards to Fire Beacon Point with Beeny Sisters, the seething, semi-submerged rocks, immediately below to the north. At Fire Beacon Point the Coast Path turns south, parallel with Beeny Cliff, towards the distinctive little dent called Seals Hole. Soon the path approaches Pentargon, turning gradually eastwards and uphill beside some terraced fields before levelling out, still going east. Now you may catch a glimpse of the waterfall fed by the stream from Beeny.

Wooden steps take you down to a footbridge and the Coast Path climbs steeply out of the V-shaped hanging valley to regain its former height. Continuing from here along the cliff

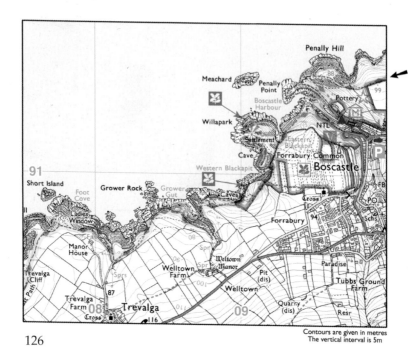

Contours are given in metres
The vertical interval is 5m

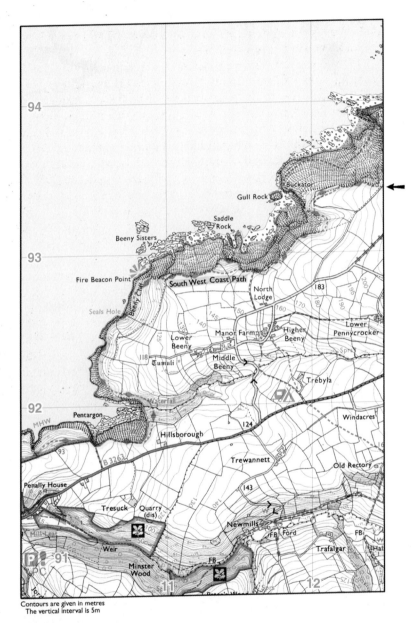

Contours are given in metres
The vertical interval is 5m

top on the southern side of Pentargon, the path stays on the outside of the wall at the cliff top, and crosses the corners of two fields before entering the National Trust property of Pentargon Cliff. Here it returns to being outside the wall and stays there until you are above Boscastle Harbour.

A Circular Walk from Boscastle

4 miles (6.6 km)

Near Boscastle, a walk of 2–3 miles (3–4 km) upstream through the meadows above the car park at The Cobweb Inn brings you to the church of St Julitta **35** at Hennett, in the parish of St Juliot.

To return to Boscastle it is best initially to retrace your steps to the footbridge in Peter's Wood, which you will have passed on the way. Cross this bridge and keep on south-east through the woods until you come to Minster Church, 400 yards west of Trecarne Gate. Keep down the country lane after this, going towards the sea until you see a stile, taking the path straight ahead where the lane turns left. This path crosses the River Jordan, and brings you out at the top of Boscastle village, which is exceedingly attractive and deserves thorough exploration before you complete your circular walk at the Boscastle Harbour car park. Leaflets available at their information centre at the harbour, give further fascinating details on the features you will see on this walk.

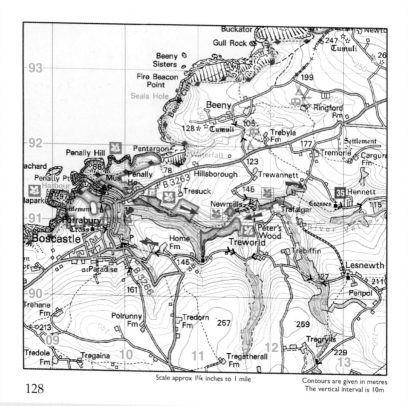

Scale approx 1¼ inches to 1 mile

Contours are given in metres
The vertical interval is 10m

Trebarwith Strand and Gull Rock at high tide.

Thomas Hardy on the Cornish coast

The Wesleyan movement in Cornwall was going from strength to strength in the latter part of the 19th century and the Anglican Church, very conscious of the competition, was keen to revitalise itself in order to counter this trend. The Dorchester firm of Hicks was commissioned to make a record of the church of St Julitta **35** with a view to its restoration, and the young Thomas Hardy, architect, who worked for Mr Hicks, came to do a survey in March 1872.

The rector's sister-in-law, Emma, was staying at the rectory at the time of Thomas Hardy's arrival. He had to make several visits and Emma, aged 29, rode her horse, while he walked alongside, to show him around the area. They would walk along the cliffs between Crackington Haven and Trebarwith, watching the surging Atlantic for seals. They walked down the Valency Valley to Boscastle and would sometimes take a horse and carriage to Tintagel, Trebarwith Strand or Bossiney.

Four years after his first arrival here, Thomas Hardy and Emma Lavinia Gifford were married, and both were later to write about their happy times on these cliffs. His novel *A Pair of Blue Eyes* is the story of a visit to North Cornwall by a young architect coming to restore a village church.

129

The Boscastle Flood

At midday on 16 August 2004, heavy, thundery showers had developed across the South West. Bands of showers aligned themselves with winds that had converged along the coastal high ground around Boscastle, creating Cumulonimbus clouds 40,000 feet (12,192 metres) high and kept them stationary for many hours. This, along with the topography of the area, was the key to the catastrophe.

Studies of extreme rainfall patterns have concluded that freak floods are more likely to occur in June, July and August than at any other month of the year. They follow a course of events categorised as 'convective'. This is when atmospheric conditions, such as a warm ground surface, typically found during summer, lead to the uplift of air masses which subsequently cool, producing cloud and rainfall formations.

It has been estimated that the Boscastle valley's catchment area exceeds 9 square miles (23 square km). The steep-sided valleys that converge down to the sea act as huge funnels and can produce true flash floods after a sudden cloudburst or prolonged heavy rainfall. During the afternoon of the 16th, an incredible amount of rainwater fell, conservatively estimated as the equivalent of 100 tonnes flowing through Boscastle every second.

The original BoscastleVisitor Centre was opened in 1994, for visitors to discover more about the area. It was run by the District Council's Coast & Countryside Service, and was managed by Rebecca David and staffed with local volunteers. After 10 years of service and over a million visitors, its interior displays were refurbished in 2004, ready for the summer season. Amongst the new panels and information boards was a segment of a 14th-century screen from nearby Trevalga church, which had been lent for display and safekeeping. This 4-foot (1.2-metre) historic piece of oak, carved with Christian symbols and angels, had with the accumulation of time turned as hard and heavy as stone and had been placed in what was known as the 'ecclesiastical' room. This unfortunately bore the brunt of the 10-foot (3-metre) wall of water that swept down the valley. The Centre's manager, who was ushering trapped visitors up the narrow ladder that led to the storage attic at the far end, saw this weighty relic float by and, despite her efforts to save it, witnessed it riding the waves out of what was once a window and onwards to the harbour. Ten days later, one of the display panels turned up on the coast of South Wales.

The torrent of water that poured through Boscastle submerged the lower floors of many buildings and swept away vehicles in its path. (Photograph by Pam Durrant.)

The story of the 2004 Boscastle flood is remarkable. In spite of the scale of the destruction there was no loss of human life. This was in large part due to individual acts of heroism as well as to the rapid response and professional bravery of local and regional emergency services. Three years later, in spring 2007, an impressively co-ordinated reconstruction effort meant that Boscastle had been completely renovated or rebuilt as we knew it .

The outstanding information centre is now in one of the restored buildings by the harbour, and has fascinating displays and information on all aspects of the flood, as well as on local history, wildlife, local activities and accommodation.

11 Boscastle Harbour to Tintagel

via the Rocky Valley and Willapark
4³/₄ miles (7.6 km)

Either go up the slate track going seawards and upwards from the arched bridge just upstream from the youth hostel, or go along the southern side of the natural harbour to the quay, beside which you will find a small rocky path. Keep well back from the cliff edge as it can be slippery. Either way, stay parallel to the bend of the harbour until you can see the former Willapark coastguard station, originally built as a summer house. The Coast Path cuts straight across the headlands with ancient strip-field systems on your landward side. These are called, locally, 'stitches' and are farmed traditionally to protect the archaeological and wildlife significance of the site. Very few such field systems survive in Britain and the National Trust ownership helps to protect them. Displays in the Boscastle Information Centre explain how this ancient democratic local food production system worked. Could this be relevant to the world's current sustainability issues?

The promontory fort at Willapark is thought to have been constructed around 200 BC, but the Bronze Age tumuli (burial mounds) just inland are probably more than 3,000 years old, and evidence of Stone Age occupation, including flint weapons and working tools, has been found. Continuing south and west, the cliff slate workings at Western Blackapit were called California Quarry. The information centre displays give detailed descriptions of how the men and boys who worked here were lowered down over the cliff to set the dynamite charges and win the slate under the most dangerous conditions. No health and safety at work then.

Keep your eyes open for seals around these parts. The Coast Path rises again, then goes down into Grower Gut, a steep little rocky valley with a stream and more clifftop workings. You drop steeply to the stream down a set of steps, cross the footbridge and then another small footbridge. West of Grower Gut, the path goes round the edge of the field to the cliff top. At the far end of this field you come up to a stone wall over which the path leads into a wild bracken area.

The Coast Path bends right, keeping to the seaward side of the Manor House and follows the cliff top to the Rocky Valley. Ladies Window is the natural archway on the western side of a small headland here. It overlooks a deep, inaccessible cove. Continuing west you will see Long and Short Islands, until recently the home of the largest colony of puffins in Cornwall. The chalet site across the bay is on the former Borough Farm, the centre of the old 'rotten Borough' of Bossiney.

Looking across the bay you can see the enormous Camelot (formerly King Arthur's) Hotel at Tintagel on the headland in the distance. At the campsite that you now reach, an ideal camping location for Coast Path walkers, keep to the seaward side of the touring caravans and tents. Just west of all this you come to the wild Rocky Valley. The rocks here have been carved by millennia of water action into a series of dramatic gullies and mini-cliffs. Further upstream St Nectan's Glen and the very fine waterfall at St Nectan's Kieve can be visited. The path goes down steps and crosses a footbridge, turns downstream and then left up the far side back to the cliff top.

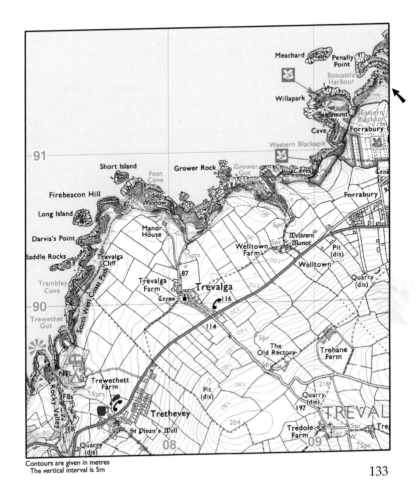

Contours are given in metres
The vertical interval is 5m

To the west of the Rocky Valley you overlook Benoath Cove and reach Bossiney Haven. At Bossiney Haven there is a pierced rock often referred to as the Elephant Rock because of its resemblance to an elephant's trunk. The beautiful, small, sandy beach here is sheltered from the wind, exposed only at low tide, but safe for bathing in calm conditions on incoming tides only.

As you come out above Bossiney Haven cross the top of steep rock hewn track, up which packhorses used to bring sand and seaweed to spread on the local fields, and minerals to the metal smiths of the known world. If you do venture down to the tiny sandy beach at low tide you will see the entrances to ancient mines. Evidence of some of the minerals they produced can be seen in the coloured deposits around these cavities. You will see dozens of such mines on the Coast Path between here and Port Isaac. The magificent and detailed displays in the Information Centre in Boscastle tell you all about the mining activity in this area and will really bring the whole scene to life in a way that you will never forget. This area was producing massive wealth, supporting Celtic princes and English kings in their territorial ambitions, supplying massive employment for thousands in the Bristol Channel, Celtic speaking, area. You can see why the power and wealth of the Dukes of Cornwall was so important to the English kings for centuries.

Now the Coast Path rises 150 feet (40 metres) and cuts across another Willapark promontory, although only 2 miles (3 km) from another Willapark, also an ancient fort. The remains are partly incorporated in the field boundary across the neck of the headland. Mineral wealth had to be defended.

The major colony of puffins, razorbills and guillemots described in earlier editions of this guide has been decimated by a cliff fall which enabled rats to reach their island ledges, and only a few breeding birds are left on isolated rocks. Boat trips organised from the Information Centres here in early June visit these sites.

Along this stretch you will hear the pounding of powerful waves against the cliffs below. Crossing a small stone stile and a bridlegate you come to the National Trust notice for Barras Nose and a close-up view of the Victorian mock-Gothic Camelot Castle Hotel. After passing Barras Gug you cross Barras Nose (NT) and come to Tintagel Haven. Keep an eye open for seals, who may come to have a look at you.

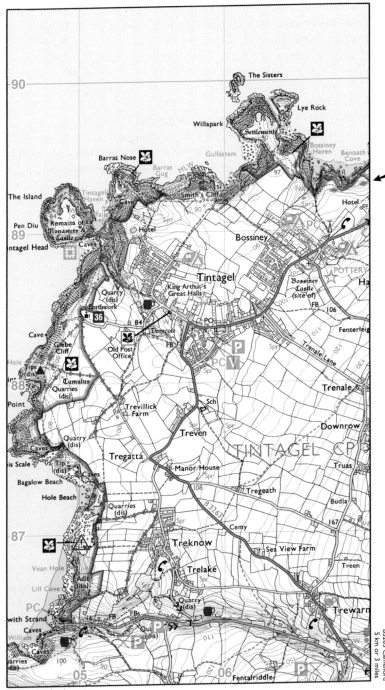

The Sisters
Lye Rock
Willapark
Settlements
Barras Nose
Gullastem
Bossiney Haven
Benoath Cove
The Island
Tintagel Haven
Barras Gug
Smith's Cliff
Cave
Hotel
Pen Diu
Remains of Monastery & Castle
Hotel
Bossiney
Caves
Tintagel Head
Tintagel
King Arthur's Great Halls
Bossiney Castle (site of)
POTTERY
Ha
Quarry (dis)
Earthwork
FB
106
Fenterleig
36
84
PO
Trenale Lane
Cave
Dovecote
FB
P
PC V
Trenale
Glebe Cliff
Old Post Office
Sch
Downrow
Hole
Tips (dis)
Tumulus
Quarries (dis)
Trevillick Farm
Treven
TINTAGEL CP
Point
Quarry (dis)
Tregattá
Manor House
Truas
s Scale
Tip (dis)
Caves
Tregeath
Budla
Bagalow Beach
Hole Beach
Quarries (dis)
108
167
Cemy
Vean Hole
Treknow
Sea View Farm
Treen
Lill Cove
Trelake
PC
Adit (dis)
Quarry (dis)
Trewarn
with Strand
Caves
William
FB
FBs
Qu (dis)
Caves
arries (dis)
100
P
X
P
06
Fentafriddle
P
X

Contours are given in metres
The vertical interval is 5m

B3263 Camelford
5 km or 3 miles

From the Stone Age to Christianity on the North Cornish coast

Flint implements show that Stone Age man was here. Evidence that Bronze Age people also inhabited the area is provided by their burial mounds (tumuli), a method of burial that seems to have lasted for the 1,500 years following 2500 BC.

The Bronze Age people, of course, exploited and traded quantities of copper and tin. Both minerals are present in Cornwall. As a result, it is suggested that there was early trade contact between Cornwall and the Mediterranean.

During the Iron Age, promontory forts were built all along the coast, and the Romans left us the inscribed stones which can be seen at Trevethey, and in Tintagel Church.

Early Christianity, represented here by the Celtic Church, was very much based on the monastery. It seems that to become a saint in the Celtic Church was mainly a matter of leading a holy life and taking a pilgrimage to convert heathens, which would have involved funding new religious settlements and churches. The pilgrim who did this may have given his or her name to the church concerned.

Cornwall has many links with the Celtic past of Europe. It was not until the late 18th century that the last person to speak Cornish as a first language died. The language is closely related to Welsh and to the Breton still spoken in Brittany, and more distantly to those of the Gaeltacht areas of Ireland, and to the Gaelic of the Scottish Highlands. The legend of King Arthur (see page 138) is shared by these countries.

Tintagel Haven

Small trading vessels would have called regularly from earliest times until the late 19th century. Remember that this would have been a small settlement and that the buildings would have been inhabited cottages.

Note the round platform on the opposite side of the cove from the castle. There are pictures of how this structure was used in King Arthur's Hall in the village. Just below it is the place where ships would have been tied up. The main export would have been slate from the former quarries you see all along this piece of coast.

It is difficult nowadays to imagine these tiny ports in their heyday, when regular loads of slates, often stacked and carried on to the ships by women, would have left for destinations all over South Wales and the West of England, and even, occasionally, much further afield.

Tintagel

The name Tintagel originally applied to the headland on which the castle stands, the area around the church and Glebe Cliff. As a result of the 19th-century fascination with Arthurian legend, Tintagel Castle became famous and so the settlement known until that date as Trevena was renamed Tintagel in order to increase the hamlet's tourist attractions. When in Tintagel, you may wish to visit King Arthur's Hall, the creation of an early 20th-century eccentric, with chivalric paintings and stained-glass windows designed and made by a pupil of William Morris, and a *son et lumière* show relating to the legends.

The most striking building in the village, however, is undoubtedly the Old Post Office, used as such in the 19th century, but really a 14th- or 15th-century house. Inside you can see the original hall and its gallery and screens passage. It is now owned by the National Trust.

Tintagel Castle

The site is outstandingly beautiful. A series of excavations in the 1930s brought to light pottery of the 4th to 7th centuries, which we now know originated in North Africa, Turkey and Greece. There is also evidence, from the Roman stone in Tintagel Church and another similar one near St Piran's Well, that the Romans were here. Cornwall was probably producing substantial quantities of tin at the time. This could well have been the export that rendered the local community wealthy enough to import luxury goods from the Mediterranean.

Clearly, these inhabitants of the peninsula, on which a castle was built at a considerably later time, were rich, and we may draw the conclusion that they may also have been powerful. The archaeological evidence also suggests that the site was deserted by the 8th century, and the first written mention of Tintagel is by Geoffrey of Monmouth in has semi-fictional *History of the Kings of Britain*, published some four centuries later in the late 1130s. Perhaps some local oral tradition that Tintagel Castle had once been the stronghold of wealthy Celtic inhabitants of Cornwall led him to link the story of a powerful and goodly king of the distant past with this promontory.

The style of the ruins suggests a 12th- or 13th-century date. In other words, the castle you see now was actually built after Geoffrey of Monmouth wrote his book. Perhaps the decision of the Norman rulers of Britain to site a castle on this spot was more an act of symbolic acknowledgement of its supposed glorious past than an act of strategic military importance. There is an excellent exhibition about all this at the entrance to the castle.

King Arthur and the Knights of the Round Table

Did King Arthur really exist? If he did, who did he represent and how has this most intriguing of Celtic legends been handed down to us over the centuries?

One suggestion is that a number of kings or leaders emerged in Britain to fill the vacuum caused by the departure of the Romans. These leaders had to defend the island against invaders, including the Saxons. Feats of great bravery were no doubt enacted in the course of these struggles. We know that Ambrosius Aurelianus checked the advance of the Saxons towards the end of the 5th century. Some people think that a verbal tradition of a King Arthur may have been based on Ambrosius Aurelianus himself.

It is difficult to be sure of any of the events of this period. Virtually all the scribes were monks, who took little interest in secular affairs. One sketchy clue is based on a document called *De Excidio Britanniae* (On the Destruction of Britain) by a Celtic monk called Gildas. It never mentions Arthur, but does attempt to give a brief history of the British from the departure of the Romans until the time of Ambrosius Aurelianus. He writes about a battle at Mons Badonicus which is deemed to have taken place at the very end of the 5th century. The document was probably written about half a century later. The leader of the battle is not named, and we have no means of knowing where Mons Badonicus was or is.

The next reference is by a monk called Nennius in his *History of the Britons,* written late in the 9th century, 300 years after the events he claims to be recording, and he names an Arthur as a victor in battle.

In the 12th century, Geoffrey of Monmouth took the whole story a stage further by suggesting, on the flimsiest of evidence, that Arthur was a great British king and a historic figure, at a time when the legend, embellished through the ages of verbal recounting, was developing and forming the basis of many literary epics. When printing found its way to Europe, the story found an ever wider audience, and the codes of chivalry helped to boost the appeal of the epic. The supposed connections with various localities in each of the Celtic countries of Western Europe are all as unlikely and unfounded as each other, and Geoffrey of Monmouth's chosen setting of Tintagel falls into this category. However, it is a wonderful story and has supplied good entertainment for centuries, and some marvellous literature in several languages. A clifftop castle such as Tintagel is as good a setting as any, even if it was not built until several centuries after the story first emerged!

Tintagel Church

Tintagel Church **36** (see map on page 135) was built at the turn of the 11th and 12th centuries, shortly after the arrival of William the Conqueror, when the land here was held, then as now, by the Dukes of Cornwall.

There is a Norman font, a 15th-century rood screen, a reredos behind the altar made of the old bench-ends, and the Roman stone in the south transept. This is often referred to as a milestone, which it is not. It stood by the church stile until 1888 and was used to rest coffins on and to sharpen reap hooks and knives. Then it was noticed that it had a Latin inscription with the abbreviated name of the Roman Emperor Licinius, who was put to death by the Emperor Constantine after a disagreement in AD 324. The stone may have been put up to mark the authority of the Roman Empire in this area.

Inside the ruins of Tintagel Castle.

12 Tintagel to Port Gaverne

via Trebarwith Strand

8¹/₄ miles (13.3 km) with seven very steep and deep valleys(A–G) to cross

From Tintagel Haven the Coast Path official route runs upstream briefly and then zig-zags right just upstream from the English Heritage shop and exhibition (south-west) to go to the top of the steep valley edge. A seal may greet you swimming around West Side Cove. As you come away from the upper ward of Tintagel Castle, you enter National Trust land, Glebe Cliff, and can in practice follow any of the clifftop routes that criss-cross the area. The official route keeps close to the cliff top all the way to Trebarwith Strand. Keep to the landward side of the youth hostel.

You may wish to visit the medieval church with its Roman milestone and have a quick look at the clifftop slate quarries (see page 146) around the youth hostel, which was once the quarry office and buildings. Between Tregatta and Trebarwith you will pass more cliff-face quarries, including Tria **37**, Baglow **38**, and Lanterdan **39**, the last with a distinctive stone pillar. The extent of medieval building in the immediate vicinity means that quarrying would have been taking place here in the Middle Ages and it continued until the 1930s. Take extreme care not to stray too near any of the cliff-faces here. Just south of the quarries you will see a seat, and soon after this the path starts to descend steeply beside the ancient donkey track from Treknow to emerge on the road at Trebarwith Strand (see page 148).

Swimming is often dangerous in this area because of the strong currents and tides. People are drowned every year because of this. In unsupervised coves, you should bathe only on the incoming tide from sandy beaches before the tide rises high enough to reach the rocks. On supervised beaches, such as Trebarwith Strand, it is extremely important to obey the notices displayed by the lifeguards on the blackboard and the safe-bathing flag system. Tide tables are on display in local public places, youth hostels, hotels, local pubs and on the internet (see page 161).

To continue south and west along the Coast Path, go to the landward end of The Port William public house and turn left to follow the zig-zagging track uphill, starting off by going some yards inland. A sharp hairpin bend soon takes you back towards the cliff top. Go up the straight set of steps to the top of Dennis

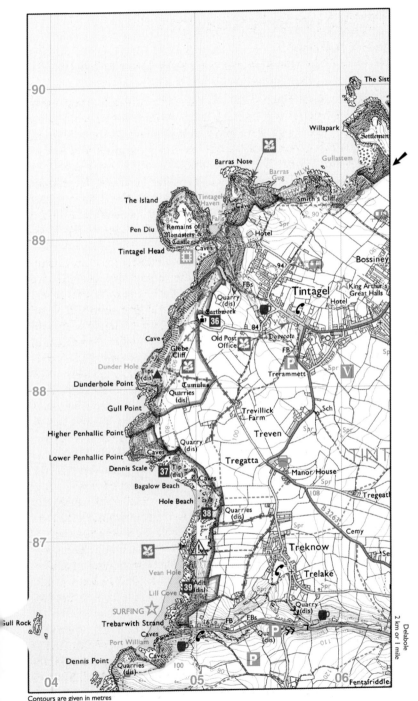

The Sist

90

Willapark

Settlemen

Barras Nose

Barras Gug

Gullastem

MLW

Smith's Cliff

The Island

Tintagel Haven

Caves

Falls

Pen Diu

Remains of Monastery & Castle

89

Hotel

Bossiney

Tintagel Head

Caves

94

King Arthur's Great Halls

Tintagel

Hotel

Cave

FBs

Quarry (dis)

Earthwork

Old Post Office

PO

Dovecote

36

84

FB

Glebe Cliff

Dunder Hole

P

Tips (dis)

Trerammett

V

Dunderhole Point

Tumulus

Quarries (dis)

Gull Point

Trevillick Farm

Sch

88

Higher Penhallic Point

Treven

Lower Penhallic Point

Caves

Quarry (dis)

Tregatta

TINT

Dennis Scale

37

Tip (dis)

Manor House

Bagalow Beach

Caves

Tregeath

Hole Beach

38

Quarries (dis)

B 3263

Cemy

87

Treknow

Vean Hole

Adit (dis)

Trelake

Se

Lill Cove

39

SURFING

Quarry (dis)

Gull Rock

Trebarwith Strand

Caves

FB

FBs

P

Qu (dis)

Port William

P

Dennis Point

Quarries (dis)

100

04

05

110

06

Fentafriddle

Delabole
2 km or 1 mile

Contours are given in metres
The vertical interval is 5m

Point. When you reach this, follow the cliff initially keeping straight on and then slightly right (south-west) to the far corner to Dennis Point. You have just risen from sea level to 300 feet (90 metres) and are about to drop to sea level once again at Backways Cove. There are five steep drops and rises similar to the ones you see before you in the 6 miles (10 km) to Port Isaac, so you should allow five hours to reach there from Trebarwith Strand.

From the cliff top at Dennis Point go through a kissing-gate and descend into the beautifully secluded and quiet Backways Valley **A,** where a small stream runs into the cove, and cross the footbridges. Then zig-zag back up and follow the top of Treligga Cliff south. The Coast Path stays on the cliff top all the way from Trebarwith Strand to Port Gaverne, but there are one or two places where some description will help you avoid landing up on the beach or going inland. There are seven descents and climbs through the lovely valleys here.

After a mile of clifftop walking on the level you drop into the Tegardock Valley **A** and 'The Mountain' – a steep little peak isolated by erosion all round – comes into sight, standing above Tregardock Beach. At **B**, you see the path zig-zag down towards the stream and cross a slate footbridge. The paths shown on the map here do not exist on the ground and so some care needs to be taken. To the seaward side you will see a path that goes south of The Mountain. This leads to the beach. Another path leads inland, upstream to Tregardock. The Coast Path strikes right south, up the steep bank and rises to the top of Tregardock Cliff, where there used to be a lead and silver mine.

After Tregardock the path remains on the cliff top for half a mile (1 km) to Jacket's Point. Continue south on the cliff top. Some of the field boundaries are extremely close to the cliff and those suffering from vertigo would be ill-advised to walk this section. At Jacket's Point (NT Dannon Chapel), you will see that the Coast Path descends once more almost to sea level in the Tregragon Valley **C**, keeping quite close to the cliff edge, likewise on the southern side of the valley, passing a dramatic, deep, surging creek as it does so. Having reached the top you stay on the plateau for only about 300 yards (275 metres) before dropping once again almost to sea level at the North Dinnabroad Valley **D**, having crossed the stream and come inside the fields. There are three more similar deep valleys (marked **E**, **F** and **G**) to cross before Port Gaverne, to complete the seven valleys you will have crossed by the time you reach Port Gaverne from Trebarwith Strand – good walking!

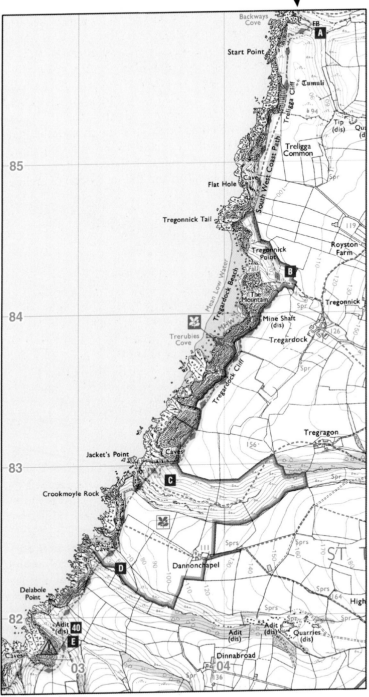

Backways Cove
FB
A
Start Point
Treligga Cliff
Tumuli
b 94
Tip (dis)
Qu (d)
Treligga Common
Spr
85
119
South West Coast Path
Flat Hole
Cave
Tregonnick Tail
Royston Farm
Tregonnick Point
B
Fall
The Mountain
Tregonnick
Mean Low Water
Spr
84
Mine Shaft (dis)
126
Tregardock Beach
MHW
Tregardock
Trerubies Cove
Spr
Tregardock Cliff
Tregragon
156
Jacket's Point
Caves
83
Spr
C
Crookmoyle Rock
111
Sprs
Sprs
70
ST T
80
Dannonchapel
140
150
160
170
Caves
90
D
100
180
Delabole Point
110
120
Sprs
164
High
82
Adit (dis)
40
Adit (dis)
Adit (dis)
Quarries (dis)
Spr
E
Dinnabroad
Caves
03
04
136

Contours are given in metres
The vertical interval is 10m

145

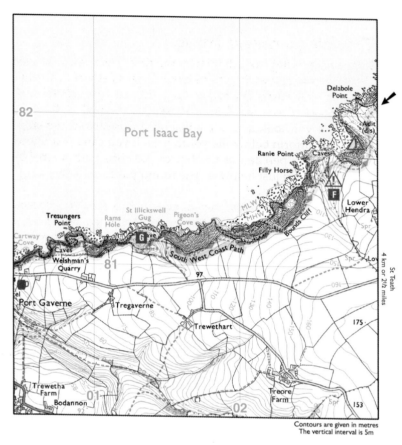

Contours are given in metres
The vertical interval is 5m

As the path rises out of the next valley **E,** on the southern side, you will pass a disused and collapsed tunnel, once used by donkeys to carry slate to the beach on the other side of this unstable cliff, to be loaded on to ships (near the 'Adit' on the map) **40**. Go to the landward side of the Adit and tunnel, and left and up to the cliff top, keeping at a safe distance.

The penultimate deep valley to negotiate, **F,** north-west of Lower Hendra, is very steep and slippery, at the time of writing, on the descent. Go inland 100 yards to cross the stream and then continue diagonally up the slopes ahead ¾ mile (1 km) to Bounds Cliff. The path is then reasonably level until you come into sight of St Illickswell Gug **G**. Here you will see that the Coast Path goes outside the fence and dips down into the deep valley below, clinging to the clifftop slopes above Rams Hole, before returning to the cliff top for the remainder of the way to Port Gaverne, a former slate port and fishing village (see page 148).

The slate quarries at Tintagel

If you are coming from the north, the first quarry you will see clearly is just below the youth hostel. Just north of the youth hostel is Long Grass Quarry and in a little bay just south of it, Lambshouse Cove, are Lambshouse Quarry and Gull Point Quarry. If you look across Lambshouse Cove, from the sloping slate platform below the youth hostel, you can see a round slate platform perched at the top of the cliff, with a smaller square platform just below it. The round platform is the site of a donkey whim.

In the centre of the circle was a post set in a revolving socket. Placed on top of this post, like an old-fashioned tap handle, would be a second bar that made the central post revolve. When the central post was turned by a donkey, a chain or rope would wind around it, hauling a load of slate or a returning quarry-face

One of the slate-quarrying platforms between Tintagel and Treknow.

worker up the cliff. In the mines, the rope or chain would have passed down the mine-shaft.

In many of the smaller ports of Cornwall you can see similar traces of the arrangements devised for pulling the ships up the beach, out of reach of dangerous waves, or for loading the boats from the quay or cliff edge.

The remains of one such whim can be seen opposite Merlin's Cave and the castle at Tintagel Haven, and a similar, more daring arrangement can be seen if you go along the narrow clifftop path for a short distance south of the youth hostel, around Lambshouse Cove and out to Penhallic Point.

You can go down to the disused wharf at Penhallic Point (see map on page 143) if you have a head for heights, but you get a better view of how it might have worked if you keep to the clifftop path a little longer and look at it across the small cove to the south. From here you can see the zig-zag cart track along which the slates were brought in donkey carts. To hold the boats steady against the Atlantic swell, ropes were connected to rings set in the rocks below and in the cliff, and the loads were then let down 100 feet (30 metres) into the boats below.

Long Grass Quarry, next to the youth hostel, was worked until 50 years ago and the quarry buildings and office are now the Tintagel Youth Hostel.

Port William and Trebarwith Strand

Port William, still shown on the maps, was a harbour from which slates were exported in large quantities well into the 19th century.

Imagine the donkeys and carts coming down and the waiting sailing boats pulled up on the beach being loaded with slates by the local women wearing their Cornish bonnets.

Mrs Thomas Hardy refers in her diaries to visiting Trebarwith Strand in the early 1870s, 'where donkeys were employed carrying seaweed to the farmers'. You can still see the cut along which these donkeys would have reached the beach, running parallel with the miniature gorge that carries the stream down to the sea.

Port Gaverne

The road by which you approach Port Gaverne from the east is the Great Slate Road. This was quarried out in 1807 at the expense of the Delabole Slate Company to enable the slate carts to reach this small haven. They were drawn by horses or oxen, and one method of braking used to slow their descent down this hill was to run the wheels along the wall. If you look at the wall opposite the Headlands Hotel, you can still see the grooves they made. The road was finished in 1860. Old photos show that many of the people who helped with the loading were women. Two cargoes a week left during the latter part of the 19th century. Records show that slate went to Barnstaple, Bristol and the Continent direct from Port Gaverne. When the railway came, in 1897, the port suffered from a major depression. The women who had loaded the slates in the past frequently dug sand and loaded it on to carts for use in the fields, and other people in the village turned to agriculture.

In addition to the slate, Port Gaverne was also a fishing village. The usual method was seining, which involved a number of boats going out to a shoal of fish and gradually working the nets around them until they were surrounded.

As you arrive at the beach of Port Gaverne you will see a house opposite called Chimneys. This was the Salting House for the method then used to preserve fish. The blacksmith's forge, where all the beasts of burden would have been shod, was in the dwelling now known as the Beach House, and in addition there used to be four cellars to which the landed fish were taken. It is said that at the beginning of the 19th century one of these cellars could handle more than 1.5 million fish during a good autumn fishing week. Most of the fish cellars are now used as holiday accommodation.

Fish and slate were not the only cargoes to be brought to Port Gaverne. There was also limestone, for Port Gaverne had its lime kiln, and the ships would also bring coal, general supplies and manure for the farmers. Port Gaverne in addition had its own boat-building yards.

It was impossible for larger boats to turn around safely in the port, so an ingenious method was worked out to pull them out backwards by means of ropes and chains passed through metal rings set in rocks just outside the harbour. This method was called 'warping out'.

Until the late 19th century, most of the slate from the massive Delabole Quarry was shipped via Port Gaverne in the summer and from Boscastle, which had better shelter, in the winter. The slate would have been exported mainly by boat until the arrival of the railways. Now the local slate quarries are closed.

The quay at Rock.

13 Port Gaverne to Padstow

via Port Isaac and Portquin
12¹/₂ miles (20.1 km)

Going from Port Gaverne westwards, you follow the pavement on the road towards Port Isaac until you come to the car park at the top of the hill and then you keep to the clifftop path, which rejoins the road of Canadian Terrace to descend the village street to the harbour. To follow the Coast Path west of Port Isaac and towards Padstow, go to the southern side of the harbour and right up the narrow lane, Roscarrock Hill, which leads up past the former Wesleyan chapel (1836). Go to the end of this road and turn right, towards the cliffs in front of the guest-houses that face you, go through a kissing-gate and up a fine flight of granite steps with a seat at the top.

Look back for a great overview of the fishing port and views of Tintagel Church and castle on the skyline. Skirt around the headland, Lobber Point, and coming through the wall you will get a fine view of Varley Head and, a few yards later, of Pine Haven.

The 19th-century folly of Doyden Castle on the Doyden Point headland.

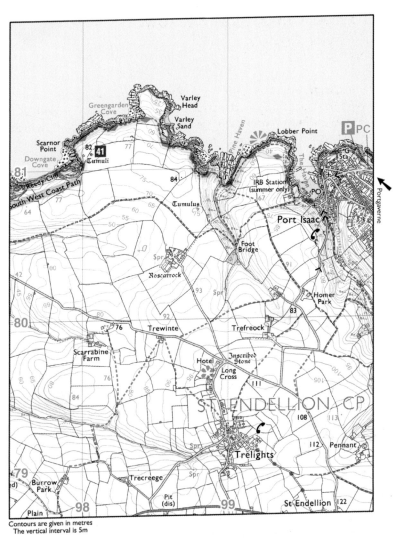

Contours are given in metres
The vertical interval is 5m

A stiff climb brings you out of Pine Haven towards Varley
Head. After passing through a post-and-rail-fenced corridor,
the path goes behind Greengarden Cove, and then round to
Scarnor Point. As the path turns west to go down steps around
Downgate Cove, note the two surviving Bronze Age tumuli **41**
in the adjacent fields.

The securely fenced path continues along the back of
Downgate Cove, with the fence almost becoming a work of art
as it winds in and out and stretches the half a mile (1 km) to
Kellan Head.

The well-protected natural harbour at Portquin, with Doyden Point and Doyden Castle.

As you round Kellan Head, you will come within sight of the natural harbour of Portquin. On the headland immediately to the west of Portquin, Doyden Point, stands the folly called Doyden Castle **42**. This was built by one Samuel Symmons, shortly after he bought the headland in 1827, as a place where he and his friends could have a good time drinking and gambling. Just behind it is Doyden House, built by an ex-governor of Wandsworth Prison as his retirement home.

You will come into Portquin between a large, double-chimneyed, stone house and a white-painted cottage, down a flight of slate steps. Make your way along the back of the beach noting the slots in the walls of the fish cellars, which were used for weighting and compressing the pilchards during the salting

154

process. Continue up the road until you see a slate stile. Turn right over the stile, branching immediately left along the fence and then to the seawards side of the prison governor's house. Alternatively carry on up the road for 50 yards and go right through big white gates, and right again through a wicket-gate back on to the official route. You can also go along the cliff edge as this is NT land. Make for the fenced shafts **43** on the cliff top towards Gilson's Cove ahead. These are the old antimony mines which, with the pilchard fishing, were the livelihood of the people of Portquin for many years.

From the old mine shafts at Doyden the path stays just to the seaward side of the field boundary, going past Pigeon Cove and over a granite and slate stile up to the rocky Trevan Point, which stands 200 feet (60 metres) high. Here a superb view of Epphaven Cove and Lundy (puffin) Beach opens up. The cove has sand at low tide, caves and rock pools, all the ingredients of an idyllic Cornish cove. The intriguing natural arch called Lundy Hole **44,** which is right beside the path, was once a cave, the roof of which has collapsed leaving only the entrance arch still standing.

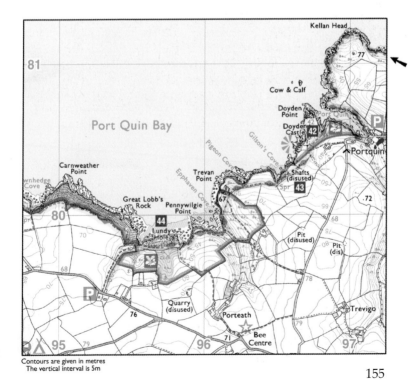

Contours are given in metres
The vertical interval is 5m

Continue west behind the cliff to Carnweather Point and round the back of Downhedge Cove. The quarry **45** just west of the cove was used for the extraction of greenstone for local building and road surfacing. Carry on westwards round the back of Pengirt Cove. Now go around the landward side of Com Head, from which there are fine views, and north-west towards the Iron Age fort on the promontory known as The Rumps **46**. Note the banks, which are the fortifications, on the landward side. Excavation has shown that the earth banks were originally faced with stone. The point where the footpath goes through was originally a complex defensive entrance which led to the headland, where there would have been circular wooden huts. The excavation also showed that our Iron Age ancestors wove the wool from their sheep to make clothes, were expert fishermen, and cultivated some grain crops. They had sufficient surplus income to buy their pottery elsewhere, and it would appear that they were buying Mediterranean wine and pottery.

On the way from The Rumps you can see outcrops of 'pillow lava', forced up through the sea floor when the rocks of this area were formed. The sea water caused rapid cooling, making the formation pile up, and the gases in the lava forced their way out, leaving holes and channels as they escaped.

From The Rumps, continue south-west to Pentire Point, from where you have a fine view of Padstow Bay. Stepper Point is the opposite headland forming the entrance to the bay, and Trevose Head, with its lighthouse, can be seen further away. Now turn south-east towards Polzeath. The National Trust has owned all this land since 1936, when a speculator divided the whole of the Pentire headland into building plots and put them up for sale. Money was collected to buy all the land, which was presented to the National Trust, which has since completed purchases of the cliff top all the way to Portquin.

At Pentireglaze Haven, skirt round the haven and join the clifftop road in New Polzeath between the bungalows and the Dutch-gabled work. Stay on the top of the cliff, following a tarmac path when the road ends and keep behind the last few houses by the small stream, taking to the road again past the shops at Polzeath. Go down a narrow passage to the right of Smugglers Cottage and turn right by a wooden garden gate to continue at the southern side of the beach on the corner by Polzeath Methodist Church. Then keep along the cliff top and cross the beach at Daymer Bay, or keep to the path in the dunes at high tide. Follow the path around the seaward side of Brea Hill.

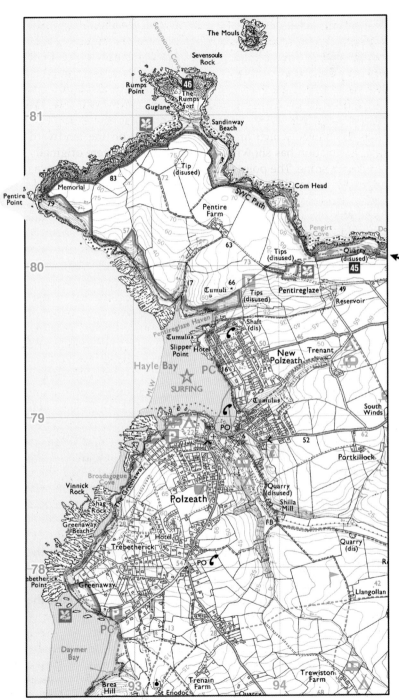

Contours are given in metres
The vertical interval is 5m

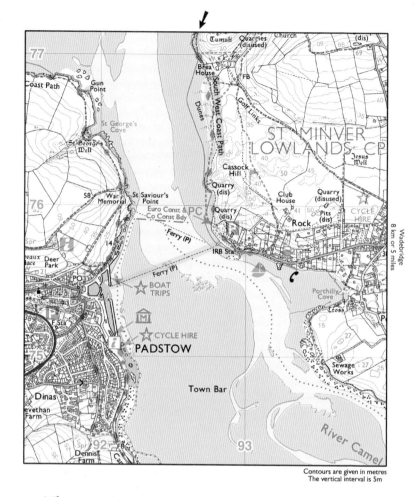

Contours are given in metres
The vertical interval is 5m

When people first came to this area, the sea level was very much lower, and only 6,000 years ago it would have been about 20 feet (6 metres) below present levels. Padstow Bay is one of the places along your walk where at very low tides you may still see the fossilised relics of tree stumps, which are all that remains of the forests of that era.

Now make your way along the beach or through the dunes until you come to the car park at the end of the road at Rock. The ferry here runs virtually every day of the year, except Sundays in winter, but when the tide is low it may drop you a little downstream of Padstow, leaving you to return along the banks of the River Camel if you wish to visit Padstow before continuing your walk along the South West Coast Path, using National Trail Guide no. 9: Padstow to Falmouth.

A Circular Walk: Portquin and Port Isaac

5 miles (7.9 km)

Park at the National Trust car park at Portquin, and walk inland back up the valley (east) until you see a green and white sign that says 'Footpath to Port Isaac 2 miles'. Follow this direction past the cottage and over a stone stile beside a white gate. Keep straight on up the valley. After 500 yards (450 metres) it opens out and the path forks left, away from the stream, towards a stile between two gates. Go over this stile and continue along the farm track which follows the field boundaries, eventually curving round to the right (south-east). Pass just north of Roscarrock Farm. When you reach the field where you can see the farm quite closely on your right, with the track you have been following going down to it, turn left (north-east) and away from the farm.

At the far end of the field you will find a stile overlooking Pine Haven. Once over the stile, branch right (north-east), drop down to the valley and cross a stream by a footbridge. Then go diagonally up the hill opposite. When you get to the top of the steep slope, branch left, slightly away from the wall you have been following, to pass a white mast on the ridge of the hill.

Make for a stone stile in the field boundary facing you, after which you stay close to the upper side of the boundary, which becomes a small sunken lane. You will emerge on to the road above Port Isaac harbour. Turn right if you want to go into Port Isaac, or left and along the cliffs if you wish to follow the Coast Path back to Portquin. Along the Coast Path, skirt around Lobber Point, then climb out of Pine Haven to pass Greengarden Cove and Carnor Point, continuing towards Kellan Head. From here you will walk back to Portquin and the car park.

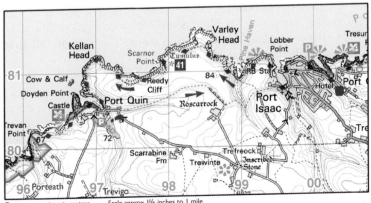

Contours are given in metres   Scale approx 1¼ inches to 1 mile
The vertical interval is 10m

159

The Rumps of Pentire.

PART THREE

USEFUL
INFORMATION

Websites

The official website giving information on the South West Coast Path is www.nationaltrail.co.uk/southwestcoastpath. This is a comprehensive information source and incorporates the latest news about the Path and links to travel and accommodation information.

The South West Tourism website www.visitsouthwest.co.uk provides a range of general tourist information about the region.

The South West Coast Path Association, www.swcp.org.uk, has news on the latest developments

For North Cornwall, www.northcornwall-live.com is useful. For countryside-related government organisations go to www.naturalengland.org.uk

Tidetables, including Porlock Bay, can be found at:
www.bbc.co.uk/weather/coast/tides/

Important Information on Lyme Disease
www.nhs.uk/Conditions/Lyme-disease

National Trust properties you may visit along the route
www.nationaltrust.org.uk

Transport

The Department of Transport website www.transportdirect.info/Transport Direct/en/ allows you to compare journey times for different modes of transport and has the latest roadwork information.

Detailed information about all journeys by public transport in the UK is available from the Traveline 0871 200 2233 or online at www.traveline.org.uk

Air

The nearest airports are at Newquay (on the north coast of Cornwall, a few miles west of the route described in this book), Plymouth, Exeter and Bristol.

Rail

Mainline stations useful for the West Somerset and North Devon coast are as follows; those that are on or close to the Coast Path are underlined: Taunton, Barnstaple and Exeter. For timetable and fare enquiries contact the Traveline (details above).

There is also a privately operated steam railway – the West Somerset Railway – between Bishops Lydeard and Minehead. A bus service connects the mainline station at Taunton with Bishops Lydeard.

For further details visit www.west-Somerset-Railway.co.uk or telephone 01643 704996.

Buses
Getting there and back
www.nationalexpress.com

There are normally *daily* express services by coach from all parts of the country to Taunton, Exeter, Barnstaple and Bude. Tickets for these services should be bought in advance from travel agents or from offices of the company concerned. For enquiries see 'National Express' in your local phone book.

The following towns along or close to the route of the Coast Path between Minehead and Padstow are served by long-distance coach/bus services: Minehead, Ilfracombe, Braunton, Barnstaple, Fremington, Instow, Bideford, Northam, Westward Ho! and Bude.

Contact the Traveline for details of services and fares: 0871 200 2233 or online at www.traveline.org.uk. You can also use the Traveline service for details of local buses along the route.

Printed summaries and timetable booklets for local services are also available as follows, or from local Tourist Information Centres.

For services from Minehead, Exmoor Coast and in North Devon: www.firstgroup.com/ukbus/southwest/devon/home/

Service 28	Taunton–Minehead
Service 31	Ilfracombe–Woolacoombe
Service 85	Bideford–Bude
Service 300	Taunton–Barnstaple
Service 305	Ilfracombe–Lee Bay
Service 308	Barnstaple–Croyde
Service 372	Bude–Barnstaple

For coastal services in North Cornwall – Western Greyhound
www.westerngreyhound.co.uk runs these services.
Timetables for all the services for the Coast Path can be downloaded, and maps show all routes in the area.

Somerset
The Integrated Passenger Transport Unit, Somerset County Council, County Hall, Taunton TA1 4DY. Tel. 01823 355668

Devon
Devon Transport Co-ordination Service, Devon County Council, Matford Lane Offices, County Hall, Topsham Road, Exeter EX2 4QW. Tel. (01392) 382800

Cornwall
Passenger Transport Unit, New County Hall, Treyew Road, Truro TR1 3AY. Tel. (01872) 322000

Ferries and river crossings

TORRIDGE ESTUARY: Instow to Appledore
Contact TARKA CRUISES: 01237 476191.
Email enquiries@appledore-letting.co.uk This is a seasonal service operating for two hours either side of high tide between the end of May and September.

CAMEL ESTUARY: Rock to Padstow
Contact Black Tor Ferry: 01841 532239
Email info@padstowharbour.fsnet.co.uk This service operates all year, but there is no Sunday service from the end of October to the beginning of April (or Easter if earlier).

LUNDY ISLAND
If you wish to visit Lundy, there are sailings several times a week from Bideford and Ilfracombe. Contact Tourist Information Centres or the Lundy Sales Office, 01271 863636, or email info@lundyisland.co.uk; www.lundyisland.co.uk

Accommodation

Finding accommodation in the peak holiday period is not easy, especially for single nights – booking in advance is recommended.

Youth hostels and campsites are noted on the Ordnance Survey maps in this guide, and many additional campsites spring up during the summer. The solitary backpacker may be able to camp in a farmer's field, but permission should always be obtained first. For details of all Youth Hostels visit www.yha.org.uk A centralised telephone booking service is available on 0870 241 2314.

There are also a number of independent hostels – an annual guide is published by the Backpackers Press, 01629 580427, or visit www.independenthostelguide.co.uk/ for details or to email hostels directly.

A list of Tourist Information Centres (TICs) is given below; they will answer enquiries about accommodation, including camping. It is best to approach the TIC nearest to the place you wish to stay. Note that not all TICs are open throughout the year. Most operate a 'book a bed ahead' service for personal callers for the same or the next night. A fee is charged but will be deducted from your bill by the accommodation provider.

The Ramblers' Association yearbook and South West Coast Path Association Annual Guide list B&Bs (see useful addresses on pages 167 and 168).

The South West Coast Path Association (see websites page 162) publish an annually updated guide available in all good bookshops, which complements this guide, and is extremely useful for accommodation addresses along the Coast Path. Free to members and you can join online.

For camping, see Ordnance Survey maps in this guide or ask at the tourist information centres below.

Tourist Information Centres (TICs)

The following centres are affiliated to South West Tourism, Woodwarer Park, Exeter EX2 5WT. Tel. 0870 442 0880.

From east to west

Minehead Tourist Information Centre, 17 Friday Street, Minehead, Somerset TA24 5UB. Tel. 01643 702624
    Email: mineheadtic@visit.org.uk
Lynton Tourist Information Centre, The Town Hall, Lee Road, Lynton, Devon EX35 6BT. Tel. 01598 752225
    Email: info@lyntourism.co.uk
Combe Martin Tourist Information Centre, Seacoat, Cross Street, Combe Martin, Devon EX34 0DH. Tel. 01271 883319
    Email: mail@visitcombemartin.co.uk
Ilfracombe Tourist Information Centre. The Landmark, Ilfracombe, Devon EX34 9BX. Tel. 01271 863001
    Email: ilfracombe@visit.org.uk
Woolacombe Tourist Information Centre, The Esplanade, Woolacombe, Devon EX34 7DL. Tel. 01271 870553
Braunton Tourist Information Centre. The Bakehouse Centre, Caen Street, Braunton. Tel. 01271 816400
    Email: info@brauntontic.co.uk
Barnstaple Tourist Information Centre, Museum of North Devon, 36 Boutport Street, Barnstaple, Devon EX31 1RX. Tel. 01271 375000
    Email: barnstapletic@visit.org.uk
Bideford Tourist Information Centre, Victoria Park, The Quay, Bideford, Devon EX39 2QQ. Tel. 01237 477676
    Email: bidefordtic@visit.org.uk
Padstow Tourist Information Centre, Red Brick Building, North Quay, Padstow, Cornwall, PL23 8AF Tel. 01841 533449
    Email: padstowtic@visit.org.uk
Clovelly Visitor Centre. Tel. 01237 431781
Bude Visitor Centre, The Crescent Car Park, Bude, Cornwall EX23 8LE. Tel. 01288 354240. Email: budetic@visitbude.info

Visitor Centres

Boscastle Visitor Centre, The Harbour, Boscastle PL35 OHD,
Tel: 01840 250010. Email: boscastlevc@btconnect.com
Displays and information about the flood and all aspects of
the North Cornwall coast, local accommodation help. Open
7 days a week all year.

Bude Visitor Centre provides information about the local
natural history of the area, combined with TIC (see above)

Porlock Visitor Centre, The Old School, West End, High Street,
Porlock, Somerset TA24 8QD. Tel. 01643 863150
Email: porlockci@somerset.gov.uk www.porlock.co.uk

The Tarka Trail Visitor Centre, Bideford Station (on the route),
Railway Terrace, East-the-Water, Bideford, Devon EX39 4BB

Tintagel Information Centre, Bossiney Road, Tintagel, PL34 OAJ
Tel. 01840 779084. Email: tintagelvc@btconnect.com

Baggage carrying and packaged walking holidays

Several firms operate guided or unguided holidays along sections of the South West Coast Path. A link to a current list of operators recommended by South West Tourism will be found on the Accommodation page of the official South West Coast Path website, www.nationaltrail.co.uk/southwestcoastpath

Some B&Bs and hotels will deliver your luggage to your next overnight stop for a small fee. Enquire when booking your accommodation if this service is available. Some local taxis also provide this service.

Useful addresses

Exmoor National Park Authority, Exmoor House, Dulverton, Somerset TA22 9HL. Tel: 01398 328665 www.exmoor-nationalpark.gov.uk

The Cornwall Wildlife Trust, Five Acres, Allet, Truro, Cornwall, TR4 9DJ. Tel: 01872 273939. www.cornwallwildlifetrust.org.uk

Devon Wildlife Trust, 35 St Davids Hill, Exeter, Devon EX4 4DA. Tel: 01932 279244. www.devonwildlifetrust.org

National Trust, Cornwall Office, Lanhydrock, Bodmin P120 4DE. Tel. (01208) 74281. Publishes leaflets about its properties along the coast.

National Trust, Devon Office, Killerton House, Broadclyst, Exeter EX5 3LE. Tel. (01392) 881691. Publishes leaflets about its properties along the coast.

National Trust, Wessex (for North Somerset) Eastleigh Court, Bishopstrow, Warminster, Wilts BAI 91-lW. Tel. 01985 843 600

Natural England. For countryside related government organisations go to www.naturalengland.org.uk/ This organisation covers the work which was done by the Countryside Agency, English Nature and DEFRA, and the site will show you the links you require.

*North Cornwall Coast and Countryside Service, 3/5 Barn Lane, Bodmin, Cornwall PL3I ILZ. Tel: 01208 893 333

Northern Devon Coast and Countryside Service, Old Bideford Station, Bideford East EX39 4BB. Tel: 01237 423655

The Ramblers' Association, 2nd Floor, Camelford House, 39 Albert Embankment, London SEl 7TW. Tel: 020 7339 8500. (Handbook has many bed and breakfast addresses: available free to members; available to non-members from major bookshops and newsagents for £4.00 or + £1.00 p&p if ordered direct from the RA.) www.ramblers.org.uk

Somerset Wildlife Trust, Fyne Court, Broomfield, Bridgwater, TA5 2EQ. Tel: 01823 451 587. www.somersetwildlife.org

The South West Coast Path Association, Liz Wallis, Administrator, South West Coast Path Association, Bowker House, Lee Mill Bridge, Ivybridge, Devon, PL21 9EF Phone 01752 896237 Fax 01752 893654 E-mail info@swcp.org.uk www.swcp.org.uk. The Association exists to help those who enjoy walking this path. For advice and practical walking information about the Coast Path

*Note that North Cornwall District is to be incorporated in the unitary authority for all Cornwall by the time you read this.

South West Coast Path Team, c/o Devon County Council,
County Hall, Exeter EX2 4QW. Tel: 01392 383560
Youth Hostels www.yha.org.uk

South West Coast Path Team, c/o Devon County Council,
County Hall, Exeter EX2 4QW. Tel: 01392 383560
Youth Hostels www.yha.org.uk

Bibliography

Delderfield, F. R., *The Lynmouth Flood Disaster*
(ERD Publications, 1969).
Edwards, *Exmoor Geology* (Exmoor Books, 2000).
Exmoor: *The Official National Park Guide* (David & Charles, 2001)
Gilman, John, *Exmoor's Maritime Heritage* (Exmoor Books, 1999).
Hall, Jean, *Railway Landmarks in Devon* (David & Charles, 1982).
Madge, Robin, *Railways Round Exmoor* (Exmoor Press,
Dulverton, 1988).
Pevsner, N., *North Devon and Cornwall* (Penguin Buildings of
England Series).
Riley, Hazel, et al., *The Field Archaeology of Exmoor* (English
Heritage Publications, 2001).
Sale, Richard, *Exmoor and North Devon* (Landmark Publishing,
2002).
Stanier, Peter, *Cornwall's Geological Heritage* (Twelveheads Press,
Truro 1998).
Stanier, Peter, *Cornwall's Mining* (Twelveheads Press, Truro 2002).
Thomas, Charles, *Tintagel Castle* (English Heritage).

Ordnance Survey maps covering the South West Coast Path (Minehead to Padstow)

Landranger Maps: 180, 181, 190, 200.

Explorer Maps: OL9 Exmoor, 139 Bideford, llfracombe &
Barnstaple, 126 Clovelly & Hartland, 111 Bude, Boscastle &
Tintagel, 106 Newquay & Padstow. *The more recent versions of
these maps indicate all coastal access land.*